WILLIAM HEIGHTON:

Pioneer Labor Leader of Jacksonian Philadelphia

WILLIAM HEIGHTON:

Pioneer Labor Leader
of Jacksonian Philadelphia

With Selections from Heighton's
Writings and Speeches

Philip S. Foner

INTERNATIONAL PUBLISHERS   *New York*

© 1991 by INTERNATIONAL PUBLISHERS CO., INC.
First Printing, 1991

Manufactured in the United States of America

Library of Congress Cataloging-in-Publication Data

Foner, Philip Sheldon, 1910-
    William Heighton : pioneer labor leader of Jacksonian Philadelphia
  / by Philip S. Foner.
        p.   cm.
    Includes bibliographical references and index.
    ISBN 0-7178-0689-8 (pbk.) : $7.50
    I. Heighton, William, b. 1800. 2. Labor leaders--United States-
  -Biography.   3. Labor--Pennsylvania--Philadelphia--History--Sources.
  L Title.
  HD8073.H45F66   1991
  331.88'092--dc20
  [B]   91-29482
                                                                    CIP

CONTENTS

Preface   *vii*

I. WILLIAM HEIGHTON: Pioneer Labor Leader of
    Jacksonian Philadelphia   1

II. SELECTED WRITINGS AND SPEECHES OF
    WILLIAM HEIGHTON

    1. Extract from *Address to the Members of Trade
        Societies and to the Working Classes Generally*,
        By a Fellow Labourer, Philadelphia, 1827   59

    2. *An Address Delivered before the Mechanics and
        Working Classes Generally, of the City and County
        of Philadelphia*, November 21, 1827, By the
        "Unlettered Mechanic."   69

    3. Working People's Movements, *Mechanics' Free
        Press*, September 20, 1828   91

    4. Report of the Working Men's Committee on
        Public Education, *Mechanics' Free Press*,
        February 20, 1830   96

Notes   107
Index   123

Preface

"The American labour movement made its first appearance in Philadelphia in 1827," wrote John R. Commons and Associates in *History of Labour in the United States*, published in 1918. Its appearance was greatly influenced by William Heighton, the remarkable labor leader of Jacksonian Philadelphia. An English immigrant, the young Heighton became a cordwainer (shoemaker) in Southwark, near Philadelphia. He received little formal education, and like numerous American labor leaders, went to considerable pains to educate himself. He was indeed a "labor intellectual." In two public addresses delivered to workingmen in Philadelphia in 1827 (later published as pamphlets), Heighton articulated the radical views of the Ricardian Socialists, including the concept that labor created all value, anticipating the labor theory of value popularized by the Marxists. In these addresses, Heighton was one of the first in the United States to point out the growth of excessive inequality of wealth and the steady impoverishment of the productive classes, who alone created wealth. In analyzing this development, Heighton assessed the reality more accurately than many historians, who have accepted without question Alexis de Tocqueville's famous dictum about Jacksonian America: "Nothing struck me more forcibly than the general equality of conditions." Edward Pessen confirmed the accuracy of Heighton's analysis in his *Riches, Class, and Power Before the Civil War*.

Heighton was instrumental in the formation of the Mechanics' Union of Trade Associations, the first city central labor body in American labor history,[1] whose appearance signified the birth of the American labor movement. He also played a crucial role in the establishment of the first labor paper in the United States, the *Mechanics' Free Press* of Philadelphia, and became its chief editor. He also founded the first labor party anywhere in the world, the Workingmen's Party of Philadelphia.

Over the past thirty years, no period of American history has gone through more reevaluation than the Age of Jackson. Yet in nearly all of these studies, an important figure in shaping the ideology of workers in Jacksonian America is conspicuously absent—William Heighton. Heighton was one of the major figures in the emergence of artisan republicanism. His writings and speeches demonstrate the centrality of republican ideals in the shaping of the American working class. Unfortunately these writings and speeches are not available in book form. They remain in their original pamphlets and editorials in the *Mechanics' Free Press.* Thus Joseph L. Blau's *Social Theories of Jacksonian Democracy: Representative Writings of the Period, 1825-1850,* reprints none of Heighton's influential writings. Likewise Laurence Veysey's work, *The Perfectionists: Radical Social Thought in the North, 1815-1860,* in the section, "Pre-Marxian Socialism" reprints none of Heighton's Ricardian Socialist writings. Moreover, David Herreshoff's *American Disciples of Marx: From the Age of Jackson to the Progressive Era,* contains no mention of the Ricardian Socialists and the leading American representative, William Heighton. Fortunately, James P. Henderson, writing in the *History of Political Economy,* Spring, 1985, notes "a recent revived interest in the work of the Ricardian socialist."[2] The writings and speeches of William Heighton merit an important place in this "revived interest."

A study of Heighton's work will do much to correct interpretations offered by John R. Commons and followers in the Wisconsin School, a process already under way in such studies as Charles P. Steffens' 1984 book, *The Mechanics of Baltimore: Workers and Politics in the Age of Revolution, 1763-1812,* and Sean Wilentz's 1984 work, *Chants Democratic: New York City and the Rise of the American Working Class, 1788-1850.* These works emphasize the importance of political activity in promoting the emergence of early trade unionism, a point fully evident in the career of William Heighton. It reveals that the political activity of labor was not an alternative to which mechanics resorted after economic activity failed. Economics and political ideas were intertwined; this was Heighton's message. So, too, was the need for labor to champion reforms such as public education. This view challenged that of Commons and his followers who argued that working class movements were distracted from their true mission by involvement in politics and in broad reform movements.

A study of Heighton's career and selections from his writings and speeches will do much to correct the neglect professional historians have exhibited with respect to the history of the labor press. Labor journalism has usually been relegated to footnote status in the standard histories of American labor. But the labor press of the Jacksonian era, beginning with the *Mechanics' Free Press*, because it had to combat distortions in commercial journalism as well as put forth labor's own position, is a valuable documental source. At best, one gets only a sketchy outline of labor events of this period in commercial newspapers. To understand how labor itself conceptualized these same events, to gain insight into how trade unionists "felt" about them, it is imperative to examine the labor press. As John R. Commons pointed out, "it is upon the labor press that the historian has to depend for real insight into what makes the movement and the special industrious institutions which have been its product."[3] Eugene Victor Debs considered labor newspapers of crucial importance. In 1904 he wrote:

> The editor of a labor paper is of far more importance to the union and the movement than the president or any other officer of the union. He ought to be chosen with special reference to his knowledge upon the labor question and his fitness to advocate and defend the economic interests of the class he represents.[4]

The first labor paper in the United States, the *Mechanics' Free Press* was founded and edited by a man who fully fitted the standards set by Debs, William Heighton.

Heighton has received public attention in Louis H. Arky, "The Mechanics' Union of Trade Associations and the Formation of the Philadelphia's Workingmen's Movement," (*Pennsylvania Magazine of History and Biography* (April, 1952), David J. Harris, *Socialist Origins in the United States: Forerunners of Marx, 1817-1832*, and Edward Pessen, *Most Uncommon Jacksonians: The Radical Leaders of the Early Labor Movement* (1967). But a study of his career united with reprinting from his writings and speeches is long overdue.

The selections herein are published as they appeared in the original. In a few cases obvious typographical errors have been corrected.

Heighton's notes are reprinted at the bottom of the page. The editor's explanatory notes are in the end notes.

I wish to express my gratitude to the staffs of the Library Company of Philadelphia, Free Library of Philadelphia, Historical Society of Pennsylvania, British Museum, Library of Congress, University of Pennsylvania Library, especially its splendid Interlibrary Loan Department, Temple University Library, Newberry Library, Chicago; Tamiment Institute Library of New York University, Pennsylvania State University Library, University of California, Berkeley; University of Cincinnati Library, and Lincoln University Library. Without the kind cooperation of the staffs of these institutions, the compilation of this volume would have been impossible.

Philip S. Foner
Professor Emeritus of History,
Lincoln University, Pennsylvania

I. William Heighton: Pioneer Labor Leader of Jacksonian Philadelphia

In a letter to the Workingmen of Northhampton, Massachusetts, October 1, 1843, the distinguished American historian George Bancroft wrote:

> The feud between capitalists and laborers, the House of Have and the House of Want is as old as social union ... It is now for the yeomanry and the mechanics to march at the head of civilization. The merchants and lawyers, that is, the moneyed interests, broke up feudalism. The day for the multitude has now dawned.[1]

In no community was this feud "between capitalists and laborers" more intense than in Philadelphia during the years 1790 to 1830.

The making of Philadelphia's working class community had its origin in the participation of artisans, mechanics, and day laborers in the American Revolution and the War for Independence. In his study, *Arms, Country, and Class: The Philadelphia Militia and the "Lower Sort" During the American Revolution,* Steven Russwurm demonstrates that the foundation of class consciousness of Philadelphia's working class, which was to emerge in full flower in the Jacksonian era, was laid down during the American Revolution. Writing of the Philadelphia militia, Russwurm notes: "At the core of their value system was the belief that they had the right to control their lives and that democratic mechanisms were necessary to implement and protect that right." He shows that the privates kept the militia equalitarian; their military organization spilled over into the civil sphere of giving the privates the means of direct, collective political action. "The Committee" of privates epitomized the "laboring poor."

Russwurm provides abundant evidence that deference was dominant in 1775, when "Philadelphia's lower sort had little control over their lives." But at the time of the "Fort Wilson" crowd action of 1779, militiamen and their followers, protesting skyrocketing prices for necessities, marched through the streets of Philadelphia to voice their bitter opposition to monopolizers, unpatriotic associators, and the wealthy. Fired on from a public house dubbed "Fort Wilson," a riot ensued, quickly quelled, but one which Russwurm points to as a "victory in defeat." When a radical militiaman on the march struck Thomas Mifflin, a wealthy Philadelphian, for attempting to intervene, that, he notes, "marked the end of deferential attitudes in Philadelphia." "Once the ruling class had abdicated its place in the resistance movement," Russwurm concludes, "radical leadership devolved on those below."[2]

The radical and class nature of the privates' orientation, revealed so clearly in Russwurm's study, was carried on by Philadelphia's artisans and mechanics. During the Revolutionary era, they had gained a much enhanced sense of dignity and self esteem. From their considerable role, both political and military, in the creation of the republic emerged a strong sense of justice and an equally ardent desire to be so recognized for this achievement. As Independence Day celebrations reflected, artisans viewed themselves as the "sinews and muscles" of the nation, the "axis of society." It was they, and not the merchants and aristocrats who were the true protectors of the country's liberties.

But there were developments that were threatening the achievements of '76. The 1776 Pennsylvania Constitution, one of the few without property qualifications for voting, was the product of radicals in Philadelphia, many of them members of the militia, and those throughout the state who had wrested control from the upper classes. The Tories had fled the city on the heels of the British occupying army in 1778, and some Quakers had been imprisoned by their neighbors for refusing to take the constitutionally required oath. But after the war, upperclass Philadelphia Tories, neutrals and patriots coalesced into an increasingly effective leadership and slowly regained their former power. Ratification of the new federal constitution, abolition of test oaths denying former Tories and Quakers full citizenship, and reorganization of municipal government prepared the way for the final conservative victory when the first state constitution was replaced by a more moderate document in 1790.[3]

In Philadelphia, the seat of the federal government and of Federalist power, the newly restored upper classes regarded the mechanics as men of inferior status and less worthy abilities. The elegant brick town houses of the wealthier mercantile and professional classes, leisurely life style, and luxurious dress of these men contrasted sharply with the poor dwellings, leather garments, and long and difficult working hours of the artisans, and formed the basis for condescending, often contemptuous, behavior. This was most fully expressed in politics, where the Federalists, led by the city's most prominent merchants and lawyers, openly maintained that the artisans, limited by their professions and upbringing, ought to willingly pursue a subservient role in society's affairs.[4]

Such attitudes infuriated Benjamin Franklin, Philadelphia's greatest citizen, and he used his pen to denounce those "of hard hearts and perverted understanding" who thought "the people must be poor, in order that they may remain in subject." He made clear his sympathy with the wage earners "in that contest, already so unequal," between them and their employers—it being his conviction that low wages were "one of the greatest evils of political communities." Distressed by "a disposition among some of our people to commence an aristocracy, by giving the rich a predominancy in government," he argued against adding to the Pennsylvania legislature an "upper house" that would represent property. Saluting the French Revolution, Franklin excused its "disagreeable circumstances," and reaffirmed his hope that "not only the love of liberty, but a thorough knowledge of the rights of man, may pervade all the nations of the earth, so that a philosopher may set foot anywhere on its surface and say, 'This is my country.'"[5]

Near the close of his long life, Benjamin Franklin sponsored a meeting on March 8, 1788, to establish a permanent society of Philadelphia printers. After the death of their founder, the members changed the name of the organization to the Franklin Society. In all of these activities, Franklin reflected the opinion of Philadelphia's mechanics. They invoked the revolutionary theme of freedom and equality to demand the same access to income, and a voice in government, equal to other citizens. They took a leading part in the Democratic-Republican Societies during the 1790's, the organizations that supported the French Revolution and Jeffersonian Democracy. Mechanics contributed half of the more than 200 members of the Democratic Society of Pennsylvania, formed in Philadelphia in May or June, 1793—the largest and most influential of the popular associations.[6]

The view that workers faced the main burdens of society while the upper classes did nothing useful is reflected by the signboard above a tavern called the Four Alls frequented by Philadelphia workmen. The signboard portrayed a mansion with four appropriately dressed figures standing on its steps and an explanatory inscription below reading: "1. King—I govern all; 2. General—I fight for all; 3. Minister—I pray for all; 4. Laborer—and I pay for all."[7]

The feeling of Philadelphia's mechanics that the arrogance and power of the upper classes were undermining the achievements of '76 was strengthened by significant economic developments. Substantial changes in the productive processes were occurring in various crafts as a powerful merchant capitalist group emerged. The merchant capitalist bought raw material, found a producer to manufacture them into finished goods, and secured a buyer for their sale. The master craftsman who owned a workshop became little more than a labor contractor. His profit was the difference between the price he received from the merchant capitalist and the wages he paid to his workmen. As David T. Saposs has observed, the masters thus could gain only from changes in "wages and work," and of necessity embarked on a search for new methods of production, "They organized their workmen in teams," according to Saposs, "with the work subdivided in order to lessen dependence on skill and to increase speed of output. They played the less skilled against the more skilled....and reduced wages while enhancing exertion." Presence of the merchant capitalist, he continues, "intensifies...the antagonism between 'capital and labor'... by forcing the separation of function and class a step further than it had been forced."

In order to increase his production and compete for the orders of the merchant capitalists, the master often cut wages and, while maintaining the traditional sun-to-sun working day, eliminated part of the time formerly allotted for meals, drink, and rest. As in colonial and revolutionary Philadelphia, the regular working hours for craftsmen and laborers generally extended from sunrise to sunset at least six days a week. (Printers were one of the few exceptions to this rule.) The actual hours of labor were somewhat less than this arduous schedule might suggest because meals, morning and afternoon rest periods and other customary pauses broke up the working day. Even thus mitigated, more than twelve hours of actual labor were required in the years' hottest and longest days. With the advent of the merchant capitalist, and the elimination of the time previously set aside for meals, drink, and rest, the workers continued to spend all their daylight hours on the job but had to work an even greater portion of the day. Furthermore, wages of the workers who were paid by the piece often fell at the same time that prices for goods rose. Hence workers were required to work a longer day for the same pay. In 1806 a skilled shoemaker testified: "I could only make eight dollars and a half a week, and worked from five in the morning till twelve or one at night."[8]

Receiving less for his product, the employer in turn squeezed wages in order to market his product advantageously. He also brought in less skilled workers from other cities, a possibility that increased with the growth of transportation facilities. Slowly in certain trades, journeymen were being forced by mercantile-oriented quantity production toward the lower class position of meagerly paid and permanent unskilled labor.[9]

Reflecting the existing trend of Philadelphians to meet in voluntary associations for almost every facet of their mutual endeavor,[10] men of a particular trade would form a mutual benefit society. A mutual fund was established into which each member paid a specified amount and from which his family would receive payments in time of need, perhaps the father's illness or help for his widow and children on his death. The advantage to workingmen was the assurance that relief could be demanded from the common fund as a right, enabling society members to avoid the degrading experience of being forced to receive public or private charity.[11]

At first masters and journeymen had belonged to the same mutual aid societies, but in the late 1790s, as cooperation between employers and workers broke down increasingly, a process intensified by the appearance of the merchant capitalist, journeymen formed their own benevolent associations. Mutual aid societies of journeymen printers, carpenters, cordwainers, hatters, tailors, and bricklayers became common in Philadelphia during the decade. But as employers continued to reduce wages and speeded up work, journeymen began to turn these societies into trade unions to protect themselves.[12]

Journeymen printers organized first. In 1786 twenty-six of them banded together to protest a reduction in their wages. They resolved not to work for less than six dollars a week and agreed to support any journeymen who was discharged because he refused to work for less. The result was Philadelphia's first labor strike, and it brought the first provisions for a union strike benefit in the country. The struggle lasted for some time before the terms were finally accepted by the employers.

This labor victory set the scene for other actions to follow. In 1791 the city's journeymen carpenters walked out in an unsuccessful strike against their masters. "*Self-preservation*," they cried, "has induced us to enter into *indissoluble union with each other.*" The sides were clearly drawn. The journeymen carpenters united after their employers attempted to reduce wages. Even worse, masters paid by time in the summer when the working day under a sun-up to sun-set arrangement, was longest and by piece in the winter when the day was shortest. The journeymen carpenters bitterly resented this arrangement which was much to the masters' advantage. They demanded that the working day be fixed from 6:00 A.M. to 6:00 P.M. with two hours off for meals, regardless of the season. In short, a ten-hour day instead of sun-up to sun-down. The masters replied with ridicule in an advertisement: "They will work from six to six—how absurd!" They moaned: "If customs productive of idleness and dissipation be introduced by journeymen carpenters, the contagion will soon be communicated to other artificers."

The journeymen carpenters lost but , as the masters feared, the "contagion" spread. In 1794 the Federal Society of Chair Makers was organized, and on April 13, 1794, on behalf of the Society, three Philadelphia journeymen deposited with the clerk of the district of Pennsylvania *The Philadelphia Cabinet and Chair-Maker's Book of Prices*. Thus began a two-year battle between the craft's employers and employees. The masters stood firm against the demands for higher wages set forth in the *Book of Prices*, and announced in the city's newspapers that they had positions for thirty or forty journeymen cabinetmakers who might need work. In 1795 the Society issued a similar expanded edition of the *Book of Prices*. The masters responded this time by attempting to break the union by blacklisting members and securing the cooperation of employers in other cities. The journeymen were left with no real choice but to fight. The union's leadership pursued a complex and sophisticated strategy, for an 18th century labor struggle. First, the workers called a "turn-out," as strikes were then known. Second, in order to support themselves through the strike, they organized a cooperative "Furniture Ware Room" for the sale of furniture, and appealed to the public to support their struggle by patronizing the Ware Room on Market Street. Finally, they appealed to journeymen of different crafts in Philadelphia and other American cities. Their 1796 statement fulsomely thanked the other societies in Philadelphia that had assisted them in their struggle, "in particular the respectable and independent Societies of Hatters and Shoemakers whose general assistance has enabled us to answer the most extensive demands of the public." They closed with a call for a general meeting of many societies—house carpenters, tailors, goldsmiths, saddlers, coopers, painters, and printers—"in order to digest a plan of union, for the protection of their mutual independence."

Just a month before, the Philadelphia journeymen had called upon their counterparts in New York. The *Argus* of March 4,1796, published an appeal "from the working Cabinet Makers in Philadelphia, to their mechanical Fellow Citizens," to "repel any attack that has or may be made upon societies of this description." The Philadelphians asked their New York brethren to declare themselves ready to assist "in a cause which will determine the independence of so useful a body as the working Citizens of America." "Thus," writes Sharon V. Salinger, "journeymen cabinetmakers did not perceive their struggle as an isolated event; they were learning that workers had to organize to secure their independence." They also learned "that journeymen and masters no longer shared the same interests and goals."[13]

The Federal Society of Journeymen Cabinet Makers not only won the strike but became the strongest trade union in early America.

The Federal Society of Journeymen Cordwainers of Philadelphia was organized in 1791 to protect the journeymen shoe workers from "scab labor." They conducted at least three strikes by 1800, the first called by a bona fide union in our history. (Strikes before this, including that of the printers in 1786, had been spontaneous.) When the bootmakers walked out in sympathy, they were probably the first to go out on a sympathy strike. In 1794 the shoemakers even compelled the employers to hire union members only.[14]

The Philadelphia cordwainers' union was also the first in American history to face the charge of conspiring to combine to raise wages. The conspiracy charge emerged out of an action taken by their employers in 1805-06 in an attempt to crush the union. The attempt failed, even though the leaders and several members of the union were fined, and it further exacerbated the conflict between capital and labor in Philadelphia.[15]

The pro-Jefferson and pro-labor Philadelphia *Aurora and General Advertiser* argued additionally on November 27, 1805: "Among the blessings which were promised to mankind by the American Revolution was the emancipation of industry from fetters forged by luxury, laziness, aristocracy and fraud." Should the masters have the right to "say to another, contrary to the will of him who labors, what shall be the price of his labor," the Federal Constitution would be "a farce" and the Bill of Rights "only a satire upon human aspirations."

Meanwhile, Philadelphia underwent the initial stages of industrialization. Commerce declined in importance while manufacturing expanded.[16] In 1805 the first really extensive cotton mill, using new machines to manufacture cotton goods, flannel, and yarn, was established near Philadelphia. Its machines were tended by women and children as well as by men.[17]

The rise of factory production in Philadelphia accelerated after the Embargo Act of 1807 and the subsequent Non-Intercourse Acts. John Mellish noted when he visited the city in 1810-11 that "manufactures of this city are rising into great importance. The principal are leather of every description, a great variety of wood and iron works, ships, ropes, fermented and distilled liquors, earthenware, tin-plate, hats, stockings and a vast variety of cloths of various descriptions."[18]

But most manufacturing was still home production. As David Montgomery points out: "The city and county of Philadelphia in 1809 produced 65,326 yards of cloth in its six factories on both hand and power looms, but its home production amounted to 233,232 yards."[19] Most production, moreover, was being done in workshops. Compared to 384 manufacturing establishments in 1810, shops and workshops numbered 1,212.[20]

Times were hard during the War of 1812 for Philadelphia labor due to serious dislocation of economic activity and inflation. Business failures and high unemployment on top of high prices made life very difficult.[21] By 1815, however, the economy had recovered, and trends initiated in the first decade of the century continued. Turnpikes, bridges and canals received legislative appropriations. The influence of merchant capitalists grew rapidly as the market expanded, and so did the increase in the number of trade unions.[22]

But the postwar economic boom was temporary. British and other European goods began reentering the American market in 1816, checking the growth of fledgling American manufactures that had been protected from foreign competition, first by the Embargo and later by the war itself.[23] By 1817 Philadelphia manufacturing enterprises were in trouble, and at the end of 1818, a full-scale depression developed. Philadelphia's leading economist and publicist, Matthew Cary, observed

> that the enlivening sound of the spindle, the loom, and the hammer has in many places almost ceased to be heard—that our merchants and traders are daily swept away by bankruptcy one after another—that our banks are drained of their specie—that our cities exhibit an unvarying scene of gloom and despair....[24]

Philadelphia employers laid off workers, and unemployment grew. Compared with 9,700 employed in 30 branches of industry in 1816, only 2,180 were employed in them in 1819. A report of a committee of the Pennsylvania Senate spoke of "A general suspension of labour...In our cities and towns, by which thousands of our most useful citizens are rendered destitute of the means of support, and are reduced to the extremity of poverty and despair."[25]

In 1820 possibly 20,000 Philadelphians (in a population of about 100,000) were out of work. In addition, even those who managed to cling to their jobs took severe wage cuts. In this situation it is hardly surprising that an end came to most of the few Philadelphia unions which had survived court decisions, blacklists, and lost strikes.[26]

The depression was relatively brief. By early 1821 recovery was underway and by 1823 a strong upswing was in progress. But general unrest in working class circles did not disappear. On the contrary, it intensified with the return of prosperity. The trend toward using apprentices or half-trained journeymen in place of skilled artisans, a trend which began with the entrance of the merchant capitalist before the economic depression, increased considerably as Philadelphia began to export manufactured goods to the rapidly expanding Southern and Western states and territories. To meet the demands of the export markets, quality was sacrificed for cheapness. An enterprising merchant capitalist could profit greatly by concentrating manufacturing in large units by less skilled journeymen. By the mid-1820s shoes, clothing, furniture, carriages, bricks, rope, cigars, brushes, barrels, candy, and hats were all produced in large although not mechanized factories.[27]

In Manayunk, a few miles from downtown Philadelphia, the textile industry became fully established in the mid-1820s, with water-powered spinning and weaving machinery, and tenements housing scores of operatives. The large cotton mill of Borie, Legueren & Keating had 4,500 spindles and 120 power looms, which produced over 20,000 yards of cloth per week, and employed over two hundred operatives. With small mills making wool for hats, and bedding, over half a million dollars was invested in Manayunk manufacturing, and the town had grown from a mere village to over 1400 people in 1828.[28]

In Kensington and Moyanmensing, textile factories also emerged, although much of the work continued to be performed by outworkers, "thousands of weavers who turned out cotton cloth in hand frames in tiny red-brick cottages lined up in monotonous rows on grid-like streets."[29] *Hazard's Register* for January 1828 listed 104 warping mills in operation in Philadelphia, employing approximately 4,500 weavers, 3,000 spoolers, 2,000 bobbin winders, and 200 dyers.[30]

By divorcing skilled from unskilled work, the factories and the enlarged workshops paved the way for the introduction of cheaply rewarded labor—including women, children and convicts—in unskilled jobs. For those craftsmen who experienced a worsening of conditions at the work place, a feeling of loss of independence or the threat of its loss in the near future probably stung as sharply as any specific grievance. The slightest speedup, the shortening of a break, the failure to allow drinking on the job, a slowing in the mobility from journeyman to master, the sub-division of the productive process—signaled the taking of a long step backward from the existence of an independent craftsman. Even in times of relative prosperity, workingmen felt an increasing sense of injustice. They resented the long hours of work, the tyrannical and overbearing conduct of employers and master capitalists, the constant fear of unemployment. Prosperity appeared tenuous, subject to the whims of a fluctuating economy, uncertain credit and currency, and competition from unskilled labor. In good times and bad times, workingmen felt that they were not receiving an equitable share of the wealth they had helped to create or, as some felt, had alone created.[31]

For a growing number of workers, living conditions were declining at an alarming rate. Forced to live in crowded dwellings, in tenements and basement hovels, they were without the benefits of fresh air, sunlight or the most rudimentary of sanitary facilities. The stagnant pools of sewage in the streets and yards of these districts provided a natural home for the scourge of cholera, which swept the city, leaving hundreds dead who could not escape to the countryside.[32]

The declining, uncertain conditions confronting workers in Philadelphia stood out in a stark contrast when compared with to opulence and privileges enjoyed by the rich in the "era of the common man." Conditions for the wealthy Philadelphians were a far cry from those suffered by the workers.[33] Here is what a Philadelphia workingman pointed out in 1827:

> When we look around us, my fellow workmen, we behold men on every side, enjoying wealth in all its luxuriant profusion—clothed in fine garments, and faring sumptuously every day; while we, comparatively, receive nothing but the crumbs which fall from their tables.

There were, he noted, "but few indeed, who produce wealth that ever enjoy it; while those who produce nothing, enjoy it with all its attendant blessings and comforts."[34]

The man who drew this picture was William Heighton, a 28-year old cordwainer, who was to play a very important role in the creation and shaping of the early American labor movement. Heighton was born in Oundle in Northamptonshire, England, in

1800, and came to the United States with his family as a youth.[35]
The Heightons arrived in this country without much means, and
William went to work at the shoemakers' trade in Southwark, a
southerly district of Philadelphia county. Here he lived with his
wife, the former Ann Beckley, and young daughter.[36]

William Heighton received little formal education, but he did
have some biblical training, and he was familiar with a number
of economic works of the time. Like many other artisans and
mechanics, Heighton was influenced by the ideas of David Ricardo, the classical British economist. Ricardo argued that only
labor adds value to natural resources and that the price of every
product is determined by the work put into it. Ricardo warned
also against overpopulation because it eventually led to such
high rents that every other economic activity became unprofit-
able. He also postulated, like Adam Smith, that the economy
operated best without the strong hand of government and with
free trade and the free market.[37]

Not everyone accepted the population and free trade ideas of
Ricardo, but his labor theory of value had an enormous influence
in workingclass circles during the Jacksonian era. This theory
was broadened into a school of economic thinkers and publicists
known as the Ricardian Socialists. They spoke for the "producing
classes," as they termed the workingmen. Forerunners of the scientific socialism of Marx and Engels, the Ricardian Socialists
were in revolt against the unequal distribution of wealth under
capitalism, which resulted in the accumulation of large amounts
of capital in the hands of the few.[38]

The Ricardian Socialist premise—that labor was the source of
all value and deserved to realize the full value of the time it put
into production—reappears in much of the Jacksonian era literature in Philadelphia. In fact, it even preceded the Jacksonian era.
It was put forth by Benjamin Franklin, the most famous of Philadelphia's artisans, in his *A Modest Inquiry into the Nature and Necessity of a Paper Currency* (1731),[39] by William Duane, the radical
Jeffersonian editor of the Philadelphia *Aurora* in his "Politics for
Farmers and Mechanics" published in 1807,[40] by Cornelius
Blatchley, a New Jersey physician and Christian socialist in *Some
Causes of Popular Poverty*, published in 1817.[41] All three may have
influenced Heighton's thought.

Although William Thompson's *An Inquiry into the Principles of the Distribution of Wealth* was presented to the editor of the Philadelphia *National Gazette* in 1824 by Robert Owen—the British Utopian Socialist—during his stay in the city,[42] Heighton did not read the treatise by the famous Ricardian Socialist.[43] Nor does Heighton appear to have been familiar with *Observations on the Sources and Effects of Unequal Wealth*, published in 1826, by Langdon Byllesby, a Philadelphia printer and publicist. But the two men's ideas overlap at some points. Like Heighton, Byllesby condemned "the existing system of unequal wealth and individual privation," and called for "such an arrangement as will secure to the producer the full products and control of the fruits of his labour, from their incipience to their consumption."[44]

Heighton was definitely influenced by John Gray's *A Lecture on Human Happiness.*[45] Gray's influence upon Philadelphia's working class movement was considerable. Between 1825, when it was first published, and the following year, Gray's *Lecture* was reprinted in Philadelphia three times. Two years later the nation's first labor newspaper, The *Mechanics' Free Press* (about which more later) published the *Lecture* serially for its working class readers. Such was the influence of Gray's tract that it was credited with awakening class consciousness among working-class Philadelphia.[46]

Gray began with the claim that "*society* is the natural condition of mankind," and that "the propensity to *exchange labour for labour*" was the foundation of human society. Gray then attacked Thomas Paine and the eighteenth-century Republican tradition for their notion that social evils stemmed from bad government. Why "do we so frequently attribute our miseries to the defects of governments," he asked, "since it is exclusively by barter that power is introduced into the world." All existing reforms, Gray argued, ignored the fundamental fact that the cause of human misery was economic rather that political in nature. "By an endless variety of charitable institutions, monuments equally to benevolence and ignorance, we attempt to subdue the evils of society, but the attempt is vain." Only solutions which "*annihilate the causes* whence the evils of mankind arise" and provide for "an equal distribution of the means of happiness to all," can ever hope for success.

From the beginning, Gray proposed no partial reform but the total remaking of society. The principles he defended spoke directly to the workingman. "Every necessity, convenience, and comfort of life," he declared, "is obtained by human labour (and) every member of the community who is not engaged in (labor) is an UNPRODUCTIVE member of society" and hence "exacts a DIRECT TAX upon the productive classes." In England, Gray calculated, the social producers received only one-fifth of the wealth they produced; the remainder went to the non-producers such as manufacturers, who were "only useful as directors and superintendents of manufactories," and merchants, who were "mere *distributors of wealth, who are paid for their trouble by the labour of those who create it.*"

Examining the income of the non-productive classes, Gray found that much of it came from rents and interest. Rent, Gray thought, violated a fundamental principle of social justice. "The earth is the natural inheritance of all mankind," he declared, and thus it belonged "to no man in particular, but to every man." "What does the landlord do?" Gray asked his readers. The answer was self-evident: "He does nothing!" Having expended no labor he could claim no right to the property he rented.

Gray found in interest yet "another mode of obtaining labour without giving an equivalent for it." For Gray moneylending was founded upon an unjust contract: "All just contracts have for their foundation *equal quantities of labour,*" he wrote. But as the moneylender performs no productive labor, he has no labor of his own to exchange. Thus he is able to lend money at interest only because his accumulated wealth gave him power over those in need of money. In a just society, Gray argued, accumulated wealth would only be used for self-support in old age, not as a means to provide an income at another's expense. "If a man accumulates a fortune and chooses to retire upon it," Gray reasoned, "the moment he ceases to do something to support himself, that fortune ought to decrease by every shilling he takes from it."

Gray called capitalist competition "one fountain head of evil" that had "filled the earth with wretchedness, and baffled every attempt to render mankind virtuous and happy." "It is *competition,*" he wrote "which fixed the quantity of wealth obtained by the productive classes." Moreover, competition for employment tended to drive wages down to the level of minimum subsistence, "to that portion which is *just sufficient* to support bodily strength and continue (the) race." For Gray, however, competition led to more than subsistence wages; it put a break on social production itself. "In the present state of society," he declared, "production is limited by *demand*." This being the case, low wages made for an artificially lower social demand, and this in turn limited total social production. Thus for Gray, capitalism led not only to a maldistribution of wealth but to an inefficient economy as well.

In Gray's *Lecture* Philadelphia workingmen found a comprehensive argument for artisan socialism, and, more broadly, a socialism of the producing classes. In place of capitalist competition with its attendant unemployment, low wages, and grinding poverty, producer socialism offered a cooperative community of farmers and craftsmen freed from the uncertainty of achieving a competency. As Gray put it, "Let us abolish (competition) and we should then have as much wealth as we have the POWER OF CREATING!!!"[47]

In many ways Gray's *Lecture* mirrored the arguments of Philadelphia's emerging socialist tradition.[48] There is also ample evidence that Heighton had absorbed the socialist writings of John Gray. In 1826, taking what he had seen of the position of workers in England and combining it with Gray's socialist ideas, Heighton reached the conclusion that Philadelphia's working classes were divided and powerless because of their ignorance of the fundamental tenets of political economy. "If the working class had always been as enlightened as *any other* class of the community," he reasoned, then the interests of working people would have been promoted "at least equally with the interest of any other class of the community." For Heighton the degraded position of Philadelphia's working class argued persuasively that they had not been as enlightened as they should, and he set out to promote a plan that would "gradually and indefinitely improve their condition."[49]

Heighton spent the fall and winter of 1826 discussing the "truths" of Gray's *Lecture on Human Happiness* and his own concepts of the problem dealt with by the Ricardian Socialists as it related to the plight of the Philadelphia workingmen in particular and in the United States in general. He discussed these ideas among friends and fellow journeymen in Southwark, and, by early 1827, he was ready to test his plan in the public arena. In two addresses: *Address to the Members of Trade Societies and to the Working Classes Generally* and *An Address Delivered before the Mechanics and Working Classes Generally of the City and County of Philadelphia*[50] which he delivered throughout the working-class wards of the city and suburbs, and which were later published as pamphlets, Heighton noted that "the times are rapidly and permanently growing harder and more oppressive." Ordinary workingmen were finding increasing "difficulty...obtaining a subsistence," he observed, and the ability of their "trade societies...to prevent or ... stop the progress of this growing depression (were) rapidly *de*-creasing." The cause of this "decline in our general prosperity," he argued, was "solely a GENERAL WANT OF INFORMATION, among the mass of the people relative to the true nature of what constitutes their rights and interests." Accordingly, Heighton devoted the remainder of his address to revealing and "exhibit(ing) the relation that existed between the (higher) classes and the working class."[51]

Heighton's *Address*, like his other published speeches, drew heavily upon Gray's *A Lecture on Human Happiness*. "I regret," he wrote at one point, "that this little work has not yet obtained a more extensive circulation; it contains truths that could not fail to open the eyes of mankind if they were but generally diffused." He insisted that "it ought to be read by every man."[52]

Following Gray, who began his *Lecture on Human Happiness* with an analysis of class relations in Britain, Heighton launched his *Address* by surveying class relations in Philadelphia. Heighton insisted that labor was the source of all wealth, that working people were "the sole authors of all the luxuries ... and of all the property of wealth that is in existence." But he noted, even a brief stroll through the city's working-class neighborhoods made it all too obvious that producers were "put off with a scanty portion of the coarsest and meanest of their own productions" and were "deprived of almost everything which is calculated to...render life a blessing."

The cause of this inequality, Heighton argued, was the exploitation of the producing by the non-producing classes of society. Heighton insisted that only manual workers created wealth by developing raw materials into finished goods. (He rejected the position of the Jeffersonian reformers who had broadened their definition of productive classes to include merchants and bankers, thereby failing to appreciate the separate interests and plight of American wage earners.) Heighton divided the "producers" into two categories—the "productive" and the "official" laborers. Productive labor was that which "produces or brings into existence some real, tangible articles of wealth" while the second "is necessary in effecting exchange of different articles, in transferring them from...one place to another, and in various modes of preparing them for man's use."[53]

Unlike most contemporary radicals, Heighton considered unskilled labor as producers in the category of "official" laborers. Indeed, Heighton urged workers to abandon all concept of differences among them and the belief that some workers were superior to others:

> We must ... divest ourselves of every thing mean and vulgar, and no longer speak contemptuously of our fellow-workmen, because they do not follow the same occupation as ourselves... We must cast away all vulgar prejudices which had their origin in false pride and ignorance, and hail every well disposed fellow-workingman as brother. The different trades can never become united, so long as the members of one trade consider themselves better than those of another; and without a union of different trades, we must ever remain the slaves of accumulators. When we can become united like a band of brothers in claiming our equal rights, oppression will begin to totter on its throne, and extortion tremble on its rotten seat. Monopoly will hide its hideous form from the glance of contempt, while equality, justice, harmony, and happiness will unfurl their peaceful banners over the community.[54]

Heighton's analysis continued with the argument that the nonproductive classes in society—the "Legislative," "Judicial," "Theological," "Commercial," "Independent," "Military," i.e., bankers, merchants, landlords, military officers, professionals, clergymen—were the accumulators; in short, they lived off wealth, but did not produce it. Wealth, he emphasized, was produced by labor but the highest rewards went not to those who performed the greatest, but to those who did the least labor. For wealth was solely the product of labor, the labor of the "productive" and "official" workers: "...these together constitute the WORKING CLASS...there is no wealth in the nation that is either created or acquired by exchange, solely and exclusively through the labours of this class. They furnish each individual in the nation with all real wealth...."

Then Heighton pointed to "the central paradox":

> We find ourselves oppressed on every hand—we labor hard in producing all the comforts of life for the employment of others, while we ourselves obtain but a scanty portion, and even that in the present state of society depends on the will of the employer.[55]

Heighton asked why it was that "we, who bring wealth into existence are deprived of the comfort it yields? Why are we reduced to poverty, slighted and despised by those who live at ease upon the products of our labor?" He traced the source of labor's degradation to the economic and political domination of American society by the non-producers, enabling the privileged few to accumulate the results of labor's productivity while they themselves produced nothing.[56]

But why had this occurred in a country that had a few decades before fought a successful revolutionary war to free itself from monarchy and establish the first Republic in modern history? Looking at the situation in the United States 36 years after the victory over England, Heighton drew a sharp distinction between the freedom said to be enjoyed by Americans under the Constitution and that experienced in practice. Of those who had seen the life of the working people and that of the non-producers who would say that "the sacred sounds of LIBERTY and EQUALITY had any *actual existence*[57] among us or in reality, more than mere empty sounds?"

The reason for this situation was "easy" to discover. Heighton proceeded to explain how the mechanics, artisans, and laborers of the Revolution had shed their blood and given their lives to maintain the rights pledged in the Declaration of Independence, only to find when the war was over that these rights had been snatched from them by the non-producing class:

> If the wealth producing class had claimed their rights at the birth of our national liberty, and maintained them unimpaired to this day, we should not have been in our present degraded condition. But for the want of information relative to their rights and powers, they were controlled by those possessing skill, who assumed the power of forming laws which have ever since chained the working class down to poverty. For the want of knowledge among our predecessors, they were led to surrender their rights to the non-productive and accumulating class, and thereby subjected themselves to deg-

radation and oppression, which has been handed down to us, and will continue to grow deeper and more severe until we shall obtain the requisite information to claim and possess those rights.[58]

To achieve the education of the working class, a workingmen's press had to be established in every city in the United States. To supplement the newspapers, a workingmen's library should also be established, with facilities for reading, lectures and debates. "Here the workingmen must educate themselves and learn to speak in their own behalf. In such an atmosphere of knowledge, they could learn one another's talents and qualifications for public office. Soon the working classes would be in a position to nominate candidates from their own ranks."[59]

The success of Heighton's plan depended upon the cooperation of the various trade unions. Up to now, he believed each had been too much concerned only with its own special problems. What was needed was a central trades organization which would be a vehicle for establishing unity among the working classes. "When we can become united like a band of brothers in claiming our equal rights, oppression will begin to totter on its throne, and extortion tremble on its rotten seat."[60]

The establishment of unions (societies as he called them) by workingmen, Heighton believed, was the "ground work," the solid foundation on which the advance of their interests could be built; with each society represented at a "Grand convention." "When different branches or occupations of the working class have formed societies, and properly organized themselves, the first difficulty in our way will be overcome."[61]

But even this was not enough. So far "we have only been lopping off the branches of the evil, which immediately shoot forth again—let us henceforth aim our blows at the root, and thus at once destroy both root and branch. The formation of societies, and standing out for wages, or hours, although it may serve a trifling temporary good purpose, is best but poor patch work to cobble up a condition so tattered as ours." The truth was that everyone who had become rich had done so "by legalized extortion: the laws of the country protect him in robbing the working classes of their productions and appropriating them to his own use without giving an equivalent in exchange."[62]

Heighton therefore called upon the working class to launch a movement to make America the kind of country the revolution-

ary workers had fought for but failed to establish. This necessi-
tated the unity of all workers, the education of working class,
and political action to restore the rights of the producers. Education must come first, for the blessings of universal suffrage was
useless to the worker if he possessed insufficient knowledge to
make proper use of it. Then must come the unification of the
trade unions of a city and then working-class political action. "If
we can unite in electing such men to office as are openly avowed
friends to our rights and interests, our greatest difficulty will be
overcome...."[63]

To describe "the evils under which the working people are
laboring" and set forth "a plan for their efficient removal,"
Heighton published two addresses in 1827.[64]

In April he published anonymously

> An ADDRESS to the members of Trade Societies, and to the Working
> Classes Generally: Being an Exposition of the Relative Situation, Condi-
> tion and Future Prospects of Working People in the United States of
> America, Together with a Suggestion and Outlines of a PLAN by which
> they may Gradually and Indefinitely Improve Their Condition. By a
> Fellow-Labourer

Later that same year, Heighton published a second anonymous address:

> An Address, Delivered before the Mechanics and Working Classes Gener-
> ally, of the city and county of Philadelphia, of the Universal church, in
> Callowehill Street, on Wednesday Evening, November 21, 1827, by the
> "UNLETTERED MECHANIC."[65]

Publication of the first of the two Addresses was financed by
Heighton himself, the second by a "Mechanics' Delegation." Both
were immensely popular among workingmen in Philadelphia,
and were, as one scholar notes, "the most literate and original to
appear on the scene at the time,"[66] while another describes them
as "among the most eloquent and lucid examples of early working-class radicalism."[67] Robert Owen, the Utopian Socialist, was
in Philadelphia in June 1827 to speak at the Franklin Institute,
and upon reading Heighton's first Address, signed "a Fellow-La-
borer" told his audience:

> I was very much delighted a day to two ago, to have put into my
> hands a little pamphlet, addressed "to the members of trade socie-
> ties and to the working classes generally...." The author of this
> pamphlet has been too modest to put his name to it; I have looked

over it generally, but quite sufficiently to ascertain its nature, and I find more truth and valuable knowledge in this little work, than in all the writings on political economy that I have met with. It is from one, who probably has not been educated in the lettered ranks—an uneducated man, except by nature and good common sense. Those who read it, therefore, will not direct their attention to the mere words, but to the object of finding certain ideas simply and frankly expressed. And I strongly recommend this little work to every producer in America—let them read and study it, and they will see their condition and relative situation in society.

Upon his return to England, Owen had Heighton's pamphlet reprinted for the education of the British working classes.[68]

Lewis H. Arky points out that Heighton's first *Address* was "a unique departure in Ricardian socialist literature, both here and abroad." Directed to the urban worker, it was "designed to operate within existing social and political conditions rather than suggesting retreat to a remote community."[69] Although Heighton defended Owen's communitarianism, he did not propose that city mechanics should leave for the countryside and build a new society in the wilderness. The solution to their problems was through a workingmen's movement in their own community, and especially through the intelligent use of the suffrage, giving their votes to those who would help them find "effectual remedies for improving our depressed condition." If workingmen could avoid party affiliation and adhere only to class affiliation, they could elect officials who would represent their interests. Of paramount importance in assisting themselves, the workingmen had to consider at once nominating their own candidates, selecting men pledged to serve the interests of working people. If this method of operation succeeded in Philadelphia, mechanics in other cities would soon follow suit.[70]

Heighton proposed the creation of a powerful central association of Philadelphia's journeymen's societies which would collect and administer a collective strike fund, direct turnouts, and recruit new members. Such an association, he thought, would give to Philadelphia's wage-earning journeymen a collective power they could not hope to have in independent trade societies. With the reins of economic power restored to the hands of the city's producers, Heighton thought, the association would be better able to support a political branch that could overcome the system of special privilege that ruled politics and to restore true democ-

racy to Philadelphia. "If the members of the different Trade Societies in this city are willing to follow this program," he declared, "I see nothing which can materially impede their progress
or prevent their success."[71]

Philadelphia workingmen, who either heard or read Heighton's plea for the unions of the city to unite in a central organization around a program of social reconstruction, joined forces
early in December 1827 to create the Mechanics' Union of Trade
Associations, the nation's (perhaps the world's) first bona fide
labor movement. Although a city federation of local trade societies from different crafts arose in Manchester, England in 1826, it
"expired before it was so much as known to a large majority of
the operatives in the neighborhood."[72]

Heighton's *Address* at the Universalist Church on November
21, 1827 contained an invitation to the members of the trade unions to send appointed committees to a "general convention" to
"hear and adopt" the constitution already drawn up by prelimi-
nary delegates, whose purpose was described as being to raise "a
general fund to assist each other in cases of emergencies." Representation from each trade union was to be based on one delegate
for every ten members. Those trades not yet organized into unions were urged quickly to do so and send delegates.

Meeting at Tyler's Tavern early in December 1827, the delegates adopted a preamble and a constitution containing twenty-
three articles and sixteen bylaws. All were ratified in January
1928.[73]

The Preamble and Constitution of the Mechanics' Union of
Trade Associations were written by William Heighton. The Preamble was written "to read like a Declaration of Independence
for workingmen," and its opening words explained the impetus
behind the formation of the first city central labor body:

> We, the Journeymen Mechanics of the City and County of Philadel-
> phia, conscious that our condition in society is lower than justice
> demands it should be, and feeling our inability, individually, to
> ward off from ourselves and families those numerous evils which
> result from an unequal and very excessive accumulation of wealth
> and power into the hands of a few, are desirous of forming an
> Association, which shall avert as much as possible those evils
> which poverty and increasing toil have already inflicted, and
> which threaten ultimately to overwhelm and destroy us.

Such an Association might not have been necessary, the mechanics suggested, "if the products of our industry or an equitable proportion of them, were appropriated to our actual wants and comforts...but this is infinitely wide of the fact." One merely needed to look around, they maintained, to see the injustice of the appropriation of wealth, especially at a time "when wealth is so easily and abundantly created that the markets of the world are overflowing with it." Workers were being reduced to a condition near to "perpetual slavery" by employers who sought to "depreciate the value of human labor" in order to "amass to glut [their] overflowing storehouses." "The mechanic and productive classes who constitute the great mass of the population, and who have wielded the power and laboured in the production of this immense abundance, having no other resource for subsistence than what they derive from their miserable pittance, which they are compelled by competition to receive in exchange for their inestimable labour," would be the first to "begin to pine, languish, and suffer" under the "destructive and withering influence" of a depreciation of the value of labor and the continuation of an unjust and inequitable accumulation of capital by the "insatiable monopolizers." Impoverished conditions were one result of this arrangement which, in turn, left workers politically powerless and unable to enjoy the freedom promised by a republican form of government. "Is it just?" the Preamble asked:

> Is it equitable that we should waste the energies of our minds and bodies, and be placed in a situation of such unceasing exertion and servility as must necessarily, in time render the benefits of our liberal institutions to us inaccessible and useless, in order that the products of our labour may be accumulated by a few into vast pernicious masses, calculated to prepare the minds of the possessors for the exercise of lawless rule and despotism, to overawe the meager multitude, and fright away that shadow of freedom which still lingers among us?

The formation of the Mechanics' Union provided the answer to these questions and to the disturbing trend toward greater class divisions. The key, they said, was working class solidarity and greater unity of action. The "Preamble" closes with a statement of the purposes of the Mechanics' Union of Trade Associations:

> The real object ... of this association, is to avert, if possible, the desolating evils which must inevitably arise from a depreciation of

the intrinsic value of human labour; to raise the mechanical and productive classes to that condition of true independence and inequality [sic] which their practical skill and ingenuity, their immense utility to the nation and their growing intelligence are beginning imperiously to demand: to promote, equally, the happiness, prosperity and welfare of the whole community ... and to assist in conjunction with such other institutions of this nature as shall hereafter be formed throughout the union, in establishing a just balance of power, both mental, moral, political, and scientific, between all the various classes and individuals which constitute society at large.

The constitution drawn up by William Heighton enabled the Mechanics' Union of Trade Associations to offer the trade unions benefits in case of strikes, either for higher wages or shorter hours. Under its provisions, when a constitutional society decided upon a strike, it was to notify the president of the Mechanics' Union in writing at least one week in advance of the proposed action. A special meeting of the delegates was then to be called, and should two-thirds of those present approve the proposed strike, the applying union became eligible for assistance from the Mechanics' Union. In cases where the employer instituted the action, the union was required to give only twenty-four hours' notice to the Mechanics' Union.

During the strike, single men were to be given travel expenses of from three to six dollars provided they left the Philadelphia area for its duration. Married men were to receive two dollars a week with additional sums for each member of their family, and were not expected to leave the city. Soon, however, bylaws were adopted that eliminated this distinction.[75]

The finance committee of the Mechanics' Union of Trade Associations collected ten cents monthly dues from the membership, each society having a representative on the committee who was responsible to the central organization. All funds collected by these bonded custodians was bank-deposited and accounted for, according to prescribed regulations.

The Mechanics' Union of Trade Associations became a going organization in early 1828, and was well established by the spring of that year. At its height between fifteen and eighteen trade unions (representing slightly over 2,000 members) paid dues to the organization.[76] It was unable to induce the older more substantial unions to join its ranks, and relied, in the main, on drawing its membership from the newer trade unions. In fact, several of these new unions were organized because of the existence of the Mechanics' Union. The city central labor body was instrumental in founding at least six new trade societies as well as a new beneficial society. The trades included tobacconists, ladies' cordwainers, printers and compositors, blacksmiths and whitesmiths, leather workers, saddlers and harness makers.[77]

How the existence of the Mechanics' Union assisted in the organization of a new union is illustrated in the case of the Journeymen ladies' cordwainers, makers of ladies' shoes. In late 1827, when the union was being organized, the constitution of the Mechanics' Union was read to the prospective members. The organizing committee pointed out that with such a city central body in existence, the fear that a strike might easily be defeated no longer was a problem.

The fear of being unable to survive a strike was a major deterrent preventing some workers from joining unions, a fear which the existence of the Mechanics' Union helped overcome. Moreover, among the main reasons for the instability of early unions was inability to survive a strike of any duration. The treasury would soon be exhausted, and the union would then be forced to yield. With its substantial treasury, the Mechanics' Union of Trade Associations introduced a new element in the Philadelphia labor scene.[78]

The Mechanics' Union of Trade Associations was not the only "new element" in the Philadelphia labor scene during the Jacksonian era whose existence was influenced by William Heighton's *Addresses*. In his April 1827 *Address*, Heighton had urged the mechanics of Philadelphia to subscribe to a workingmen's library and a newspaper. In September 1827 the library was established in North Alley, and opened its door to the workingmen. Called the Mechanics' Library Company, the institution became a clearinghouse of ideas, a forum for discussion, and a meeting place for all regardless of trade. It was, in short, an institution for the "diffusion of knowledge," a place where mechanics might equip themselves for their "proper station in society."[79]

By November 1827, the Library already had sixty members, each of whom paid a fee of one dollar, and over a hundred volumes, and many periodicals which could be read in its single room during the long hours the library was open. A regular feature was the Wednesday evening debate where subjects designed to encourage the growth of the workingmen's movement were discussed. Among the topics debated were: "Is an increase of industry and economy among the working classes calculated to meliorate their condition?" "Should Money Be Eliminated from the Economy and Barter Stores substituted instead?"[80]

All ten members of the Library's first Board of Directors were active in Philadelphia's workingmen's movement, and included a chairmaker, a tailor, a plasterer, a shoe storekeeper, and a hat storekeeper.[81] William Heighton was the secretary, and it was he who kept the public informed of the Library's progress.[82]

One of the main functions of the Mechanics' Library was to edit and publish a "Free Press" for the education of Philadelphia's mechanics. In 1797 William Manning, a poor, untutored Massachusetts farmer proposed in his *Key of Liberty* the organization of a nationwide "Labouring Society" for all Americans who worked for a living. The most important function of this society would be the publication of a monthly magazine and weekly newspaper. The government, Manning thought, should support the papers in behalf of the public welfare.[83]

Nothing came of Manning's idea, but something did come of William Heighton's call for a labor press. The project was begun in November 1827, and in January 1828, the first issue of the *Mechanics' Free Press* was published. The first issue extant is that of April 12, 1828.

The *Mechanics' Free Press* had already been preceded by two papers that directed their attention to the workingmen. The first weekly paper to do so in the United States was the *Journeymen's Mechanics' Advocate*, which began publication in Philadelphia around June 1827, but ceased after a few months. Its successor was the *Mechanics' Gazette*, which like the *Advocate*, sought to build circulation among workingmen and act as their organ. But both were commercial papers, and neither was edited by workers.[84] The *Mechanics' Free Press* was the first newspaper in America for workers and edited entirely by workingmen, and while the Journeymen bricklayers endorsed the *Journeymen Mechanics' Advocate* and recommended it "to the patronage of journeymen mechanics generally," the *Mechanics' Free Press* was the official organ of the Mechanics' Union of Trade Association.[85]

The prospectus of the *Mechanics' Free Press*, written by Heighton, described it as a paper which would not "be got up in the usual way," but would be edited by a committee of workingmen from the Mechanics' Library Company. The workers could be sure that the editors of the paper would never betray them.[86] The prospectus listed no names as editors. But it became known almost immediately that William Heighton was the chief editorial writer, and he was assisted by a board which included the printers, Thompson and Garden. The subscription would be $2 per annum, payable quarterly in advance. If the subscriptions exceeded expectations, the price would be reduced. "Relying with confidence on an ability to perform all we have promised,' the prospectus concluded, "We respectfully solicit those who feel an interest in the plan to aid and assist us with their patronage and support."[87]

A four-page, five-column (later six-column) weekly, the *Mechanics' Free Press* carried on the masthead the information that it was "A Journal of Practical and Useful Knowledge," edited and published by a committee of the Mechanics' Library Company of Philadelphia. It headed its editorial columns with an eagle carrying arrows in one claw, a branch of flowers and fruit in the other claw. It lasted from 1828 to 1835, but Heighton, who left Philadelphia in 1830, played no role in the paper after that. It had and average weekly circulation of about 1,500 to 2,000, when even major Philadelphia papers claimed only 4,000.[88]

In an editorial in the *Mechanics' Free Press* of April 12, 1828, "TO OUR PATRONS," Heighton wrote:

...To our patrons we return our grateful acknowledgements for their prompt and generous support, at the same time indulging the hope, that our future exertions will warrant a continuance of their favour. To the working public generally we appeal for support, in consideration of the fact, that this is the *only journal* now in existence in this city *devoted to their interest.* True: many have built much on the *Mechanics' Gazette,* and we had ourselves anticipated something; but certain movements of late have withheld our hopes in that quarter, and we now feel that we stand ALONE. We cannot but sincerely regret the falling off of the *Gazette,* in its late deviation from its avowed objects, and although the existence of that paper presented an almost insurmountable obstacle to our struggle for existence, we had consoled ourselves with the cheering promise of its proposed usefulness,—to what extent fond hope has been realized, we leave our fellow-labourers to determine. Thus unaided and alone with the torrent of popular prejudice against us—will our fellow labourers desert us? Shall it be said, that we cannot, or perhaps will not support a journal of our own, in a city where our class is so very numerous? But we have no fears on this ground— and may we not be permitted to hope, that the day is not far distant, when a greatly increased patronage shall enable us to enlarge our sheet, improve its character and workmanship, and render it a journal altogether creditable to that class for whom alone it exists. If so, we shall smile with contempt upon the infuriated bigot, and unprincipled aristocrat, although we are not ignorant of the pitiful means by which they are now attempting our destruction.

In the issue of August 29, on "Our Grammar," Heighton wrote:

A correspondent finds fault with our grammar! "Hear O heaven, and be astonished O earth!" In an advertisement of our company, now on the fourth page, headed "Mechanics' Library Company" we have mistaken "advantages" for the nominative, whereas *library* is the nominative; which, our correspondent most justly observes, "shows a great want of syntactical precision." He then suggests that we throw the blame on the compositor; but this we have no inclination to do; it was most likely printed, as written. We wish to know which of our company wrote this abominably ungrammatical sentence, we would vote in our publication committee, that his name should be made known, that the other members might not lie under the imputation. It is certainly laughable enough, that we mechanics should blunder so gregariously in grammar, when we have such correct examples before our eyes, in presidents, congressmen, judges, lawyers, squires and even some preachers. We will go further—the remarkable "syntactical precision" used by some of our brother editors, should create in our breast some desire to become acquainted with concord and government—conjugations and declinations—antecedents, nominatives, objectives, tenses, moods, degrees, exclamations, &c. &c.

In the issue of November 7, 1829, Heighton welcomed the advent of the New York *Working Men's Advocate* in an editorial entitled "Progress of the Working Men's Cause":

We have received the first No. of a new weekly paper, published in the city of N.Y. entitled the "Working Man's Advocate."[89] From the hasty perusal we have been able to give it, we find that the matter it contains is in accordance with the great principles we advocate;

and from the talents displayed in the number before us, we have no doubt they will be ably and judiciously maintained.

Our brethren in New York have taken us by surprise: while fears were expressed by some that they were loitering behind, we find them suddenly appearing alongside, and not a whit behind us in the advocacy of the all-important cause which we have been labouring with much difficulty these last two years to accomplish...We heartily wish our friends success in the good cause they have so nobly undertaken.

In the issue of July 24, 1830, one of the last he edited, Heighton appealed "To Advertisers, &c."

The extended and increasing circulation of *The Mechanics' Free Press*, render it a valuable medium through which buyers and sellers can make known their wishes. Nearly 2,000 copies are distributed weekly through the city and suburbs of Philadelphia; and it is chiefly confined to Mechanics and Manufacturers.

In its issue of December 20, 1828, *The Correspondent*, a Deist journal published in New York City, suggested that the *Mechanics' Free Press* "ought to be in the hands of every mechanic in the United States." In 1829, the *Marietta Pioneer*, published in Ohio, declared:

There is a paper now published weekly in the city of Philadelphia, called "The Mechanics' Free Press," which should be in the possession of every mechanic who takes a city paper. It is devoted to the discussion of all subjects connected with the happiness and interest of labourers, mechanics and poor men generally, and is the warm opponent of all aristocratic and oppressive monied individuals, institutions and societies....[90]

This is an accurate summary of the contents of America's first labor paper. Assaults were regularly launched against "the aristocracy of wealth, professional claims of rank, or the power of overgrown capitalists." Laborers were assured the paper would "support their rights, advance their interests," and elevate them to a position in society which they were "designed to occupy."[91]

The paper was more than a reporter of news; it was a forum for the views of its correspondents, many of whom were mechanics or other workers, and a guide for the economic and political action of Philadelphia labor. Most of the time William Heighton, as chief editor, kept himself well to the background, allowing the correspondents and reprints from other papers to appear for him on certain issues where no editorials appeared.

But he did comment occasionally on letters received and published, as well as those received and not inserted. When the paper carried an attack on woman's rights, it received a vigorous reply from "A Female Subscriber," who questioned the editor's judgment and pretension to progressivism by publishing the defense of male supremacy.[92]

By reprinting "The Dying Slave," originally published in the Abolitionist weekly *The Genius of Universal Emancipation*, and by commenting caustically on a letter in the Columbian *Telegraph* urging laws to prevent slaves from being taught to read and write, Heighton showed his sympathy with the slaves.[93] But the *Mechanics' Free Press* never went beyond this indirect expression of hostility to slavery; never directly attacked the "Peculiar Institution," or called for its abolition.

Although the Mechanics' Union of Trade Associations concerned itself only with the skilled artisans, and overlooked unskilled and factory workers, the *Mechanics' Free Press* did not. Heighton had denounced working-class snobbishness in his *Addresses*, and as editor, he was particularly concerned about the plight of the unskilled, especially factory workers and female laborers. He published exposés of the terrible exploitation of seamstresses and tailoresses, the letters of protesting operatives, and editorialized in their behalf. When the wages of factory hands were cut 25 percent in September 1828, the *Mechanics' Free Press* supported their strike against the reduction in wages, and Heighton formed a committee of his own union, The United Brotherhood Society of Journeymen Cordwainers to gather support for the Manayunk spinners.[94]

But the plight of Black workers in Philadelphia elicited no comment. The first labor paper paid no attention to the displacement of Black workers in skilled occupations by immigrant workers who assumed that their white skin entitled them to these jobs, and used force to assert their "right." Free Black workers were reduced to the most menial of occupations—laborers, mariners, carters, and other unskilled occupations. But none of this appeared in the *Mechanics' Free Press*. Indeed, not a word on the Black worker appeared in the *Mechanics' Free Press* or in any of Heighton's speeches, editorials or comments.

Notices of union meetings and advertisements filled a number of columns, making the *Mechanics' Free Press* a most valuable source for the activities of the Philadelphia labor movement in the Jacksonian era. Most of the advertisements appeared on the fourth page, and were generally of the sort found in any of the contemporary commercial papers. The first column of page four was devoted each week to "POETRY." Above the poem would often appear the notice "ORIGINAL" or "For the *Mechanics' Free Press.*" Most of the poems dealt with issues of concern to workingmen. The first labor paper was thus an important vehicle for working class culture.

The main purpose of the *Mechanics' Free Press* was to carry forward the enlightenment of the city's working class. In the three and a half years of its existence, Philadelphia journeymen could read in the *Free Press* a complete reprint of Gray's *A Lecture on Human Happiness,* articles on Pestalowzian educational reform, and Heighton's articles on artisan socialism.[95]

In his 1827 *Addresses* and in editorials in the *Mechanics' Free Press,* Heighton pointed out that the blessings of universal suffrage had so far gained the workingmen very little. On the contrary, the men in office were individuals whose interest was "at variance" with that of the working class. The manner in which memorials of working people were treated in the councils of the city of Philadelphia and in the Pennsylvania legislature "show us clearly that we may expect neither favor nor affection, neither equal laws nor justice from any political party who may ascend into power."[96] Nor was this surprising, for the candidates for public office were "taken entirely from the class of citizens who are rich themselves or dominated by the rich." Not until the workers formed their own political parties and selected men from their own class to be their candidates would this situation change.[97]

"A new distinction of parties is about to originate," Heighton announced in the summer of 1828, "involving, on the one side the *industrious classes,* and on the other, the *idle and unproductive.*" The new standard of politics to which he referred was the world's first Workingmen's Party to represent the interest of the city's working classes.[98] "The truth is," Heighton declared to a meeting of Southwark journeymen, "the Working People of this country have never yet been *faithfully* represented in their legislative councils by those to whom they have given *their* suffrages." He cautioned his fellow workingmen that "we have permitted the wealthy and the proud, whose INTEREST it has been, and is, to render us poor and degraded, to NOMINATE, as candidates for public offices, individuals of their own stamp."[99] The result of this, he told his audience, was the "charters, statutes, and enactments, passed from session to session (of the legislature), for the exclusive advancement and benefit of Banking, Insurance and Mercantile, *master* Manufacturing, Landed, and other monied, monopolizing, and speculating institutions and interests." These interests, Heighton warned, were "under the fostering wing of legislative protection ... accumulating their annual millions from the toils and labours of the Operative classes."[100]

It was a well-known fact, Heighton argued, that "the interest of the labourer had never been efficiently recognized by the legislators." Nevertheless, the workingmen had blindly supported such men at the polls only to see their interests neglected, and along with this "a decline in their rights and privileges."[101]

To strengthen his argument, Heighton reprinted the section of his pamphlet *An Address to the Trade Societies and to the Working Class Generally* dealing with "LEGISLATORS" in the *Mechanics' Free Press* of June 12, 1828. In explaining the reprint, Heighton wrote in an editorial in the same issue:

In compliance with the request of several friends, we have this week given place to an extract, headed "Legislators," on the nature and character of our popular elections, from a pamphlet published in April of last year.[102] We feel the more willing to do this, as the pamphlet in question has received but a limited circulation, only 500 copies of it having been printed; and more especially as the present period appears peculiarly favourable to call the special attention of our fellow mechanics to this most important subject; seeing that they are now becoming very generally animated with an ardent desire to acquaint themselves with, and to enjoy all the benefits resulting from the right of suffrage. We rejoice that such a spirit (which is at once the offspring and the evidence of a generally improving intellect), has gone forth among them; and we trust that the day is not distant, when they will assume the right chartered to them by the constitution, of nominating as well as electing their public officers.

Why should the working classes leave, any longer, so all-important a duty as that involved in the *first* choice of representatives, to be performed by an interested few, among the idle and useless classes? They cannot rationally expect to participate in a full share of information and science, or to enjoy an equal distribution of the blessings that flow from their labours, while they place all their destinies in the hands of men whose affluence proceeds from their toils and privations, and whose dignity and greatness are almost totally dependent on the continuance of their ignorance and degradation.

To increase the prosperity, and improve the condition of the working classes, is incompatible with the interests of great landed proprietors, capitalists and speculators; and the due administration of justice, and general advancement of morals, by annihilating the causes of litigation, is inimical to the personal aggrandizement of lawyers.

Once again Philadelphia workingmen read that legislators "constitute in point of intelligence and influence, the most powerful class of men in the nation," and that while elected *"by the great body* of the people as THEIR REPRESENTATIVES," they served only the interests of the non-producers, the groups in society opposed to the working class, and that this would continue "until we have men of our own nominating, men whose interests are in *unison* with ours...

The Philadelphia Working Men's Party was the first of many in the United States in the Jackson era. Independent workers' political parties were organized in 61 cities and towns during the years 1828 to 1834, and in communities where no independent parties were formed, this movement stimulated the growth of mechanics' clubs which advocated legislation for the benefit of wage earners.[103] Along with the rise of the workers' parties went the formation of labor papers. Almost 50 labor weeklies were published in cities and towns during the years 1827-1832.[104]

The program of the Philadelphia Working Men's Party, much of it the contributions of William Heighton, was to become the basis for the platform of the labor parties everywhere. It included, first and foremost, a call for a free, tax-supported school system to replace the hated "pauper schools." The additional reforms demanded during the life of the Party included: passage of a mechanics' lien law; abolition of imprisonment for debt; abolition of all licensed monopolies; an entire revision or abolition of the prevailing militia system; a less expensive legal system; equal taxation on property; no legislation on religion; the election of all officers by the vote of the people. In addition, the Philadelphia Working Men's Party intermittently protested against the unsanitary and overcrowded housing conditions of workingmen; the high cost of living; the long hours, low wages, and poor working conditions of labor, as well as the low esteem in which manual work was held; the hostility of the major parties toward labor; the invocation of the conspiracy doctrine against labor unions; insufficient "hydrant water for the accommodation of the poor," and "the failure of the city to clean the streets in the remote sections of the city where the workingmen reside."[105]

The Philadelphia Working Men's Party called for greater democracy in government. It demanded the elimination of property qualifications for holding office, and condemned the caucus system of nominating candidates as a method through which a handful of party leaders controlled the selection of men for public office. It also opposed indirect elections, for "there should be no intermediate body of men between the electors and the candidates (and) that all important officials be elected directly by the people.[106]

All in all, the Philadelphia Working Men's Party was bent upon realizing the principles of the Declaration of Independence by changing economic and social conditions. "The objects we have in view," it declared, "are hallowed by the sympathy of patriotism—it is the finish of the glorious work of the Revolution." It was a movement which "Jefferson, if he yet lived, would receive and recognize as his own." For he would be the first to recognize "that the cause of the workingmen is the cause of the country."[107]

The key demand of the Working Men's Party, and one common to all of the labor parties, was the establishment of a system of public education for the children of the poor as well as the rich. It was not a new demand. In the 1790s, the mechanics and laborers of the Democratic-Republic Societies had demanded public education. Since that time, much had happened to convince Philadelphia workingmen that the issue was of the utmost importance. They saw their children growing up in ignorance. The few schools that existed for the children of the poor carried the pauper taint, and so, few children attended the hated city schools. Philadelphia workingmen demanded education for their children not as "a grace and bounty of charity," but as "a matter of right and duty." They were convinced that without education their children would never be able to take their rightful place in American society. For these children as for all poor people, the "land of opportunity" would remain but a meaningless phrase.[108]

"Lack of education deprives the poor from representation in government," the *Mechanics' Free Press* argued. Philadelphia workers declared that only by procuring free education for all children would workingmen be able to preserve the republic "from the dangers of foreign invasion and domestic infringement," and a working class poet wrote in the *Mechanics' Free Press:*

> Lawns may bloom, and cities flourish,
> And your ship invade the sea;
> Schools alone, the mind can nourish,
> That will save your liberty.[109]

A committee of workingmen investigating the state of public education in Pennsylvania made the following observation: "The original element of despotism is a monopoly of talent, which consigns the multitude to comparative ignorance, and secures the balance of knowledge on the side of the rich and rulers—this monopoly should be broken up, and...the means of equal knowledge (the only security for equal liberty), should be rendered, by legal provision, the common property of all classes."[110]

As if to rub salt into the wounds of the working people, the legislature appropriated funds for the improvement of colleges and universities, which the sons of the poor were unable to attend. "Funds thus expended," exploded the *Mechanics' Free Press* in wrath, "may serve to engender an aristocracy of talent, and place knowledge, the chief element of power, in the hands of the privileged few; but can never secure the common prosperity of a nation nor confer intellectual as well as political equality on a people."[111]

As more workingmen denounced the inadequate school system of Philadelphia and indicated their reluctance to inflict their children with the stigma of being "charity" students, the movement for public schools grew. In 1827 the Pennsylvania Society for the Promotion of Public Schools was founded by Robert Vaux and a group of associates, including Matthew Carey. Its purpose was to offer free elementary education at public expense for all children in the state, the schools to be supported by an education tax. The Society drew up a model education bill designed to supersede the educational law of 1809, which placed the public schools in the category of pauper relief. Workingmen supported the Society's efforts, and in 1829 organized their own society, the

Association for the Protection of Industry and the Promotion of Popular Instruction, to both preserve the journeymen system and further the cause of public education.[112]

Imprisonment for debt was another practice that angered the poor of Philadelphia. It was estimated in 1829 that more than 75,000 people were in prison in the United States because of debts, more than half of them for sums of less than twenty dollars. *Hazard's Register* reported that from June 6, 1829, until February 24, 1830, 817 persons were imprisoned for debt in Philadelphia, 233 of whom for debts below $5.00.[113]

The compulsory militia system intensely angered the Philadelphia workingmen, and they rallied to secure its abolition. According to this system, all citizens had to turn out at stated periods, usually three times a year, to parade and drill. Failure to report brought a fine of $12.00 annually, and failure to pay the fine brought a jail sentence. This requirement was no burden to the wealthy who avoided duty by paying the fine, but to workers who could not pay or be absent from work, it was a heavy burden. They were, ready to defend their country, but they saw little value in the "expensive and useless machinery of pageantry and parade."[114]

When an employer went bankrupt, the workers usually received no part of the wages due them, and at a time when wages were often paid on a monthly, or even semi-annual basis, some employers found it profitable to go into bankruptcy in order to pocket unpaid wages. Petitions to the legislature over the course of thirty years having brought no redress, the workers decided to use their power at the polls to obtain the much needed mechanics' lien law.[115]

Opposition to chartered monopolies ranked high among the grievances set forth in the declaration of the Working Men's Party of Philadelphia. The worst of all monopolies, according to the workingmen, was the banking monopoly. They feared that banking monopolies would grow in power and influence until they would control American economic and political life. With unlimited sources of capital in their hands, bankers constituted a small and powerful group. Soon no amount of opposition would succeed in unseating them; hence action was imperative before they could enrich themselves to "perpetuate an aristocracy which eventually may shake the foundations of our liberties and entail slavery upon our posterity."[115] In addition to the general fear of financial monopolies, the workingmen had specific grievances against the banks. Wages at this time were usually paid in bank notes whose value fluctuated in relation to the solvency of the bank at issue. Whereas merchants took bank notes only at discount, workers were forced to take them at face value. Hence the workers' purchasing power varied from week to week and from day to day.[116]

Workingmen demanded the abolition of bank notes, and the payment of wages in specie. A number of resolutions adopted by the Working Men's Party called for outright repeal of charters granted to banks. Others demanded the passage of laws limiting the power of these financial institutions. A few even advanced the demand that the government should take over control of banking and issuing of currency, thereby providing a stabilized currency system which would check inflation and at the same time prevent any domination of political life by banking monopolies.[117]

Unequal taxation was another grievance. The Working Men's Party wished to replace taxes on the necessaries of life by "fair income or property tax (which) would bear much equally or impartially on all the people." On the other hand, they advocated that bonds and mortgages be taxed and exemption of church property from taxation be ended, not only because it was a form of special privilege similar to monopolistic charter, but because it also represented the dangerous "connection of church and state."[118] However, when this provoked the attack that the Working Men's Party was opposed to God and religion, the demand was abandoned.

Several things should be noted about the program of the Working Men's Party of Philadelphia, and that also reveal William Heighton's political thought. For one thing, the program reflected Heighton's emphasis upon labor achieving an improved status in society. For another the demands of the Working Men's Party were not of interest solely to workers. A number were supported by men and groups outside the labor movement. Imprisonment for debt, for example, affected businessmen who suffered under existing bankruptcy laws, and sought repeal of the vicious practice, as well as the workingmen.[119] A public, tax-supported system of education was supported on broad humanitarian grounds by others besides workers. However, Heighton's writings on this issue and the activity of the Working Men's Party of Philadelphia certainly contradict the revisionist argument that much of the impetus for public, tax-supported schools came not from the urban workers but from the upper and middle class.[120]

A few months after it was organized, the bylaws of the Mechanics' Union of Trade Associations were amended to provide that three months prior to general elections, the membership should "nominate as candidates for public office such candidates as shall pledge themselves to support and advance the interests and enlightenment of the working classes ... and to recommend to the members of the represented societies, and to the working classes generally, to support and promote the interests of the same (candidates) at the next ensuing general election." In the nomination, "Party politics shall be entirely out of the question...."[121]

Heighton had drawn up the amended bylaw, and it was he who wrote the resolution introduced at a general meeting in August 1828, of the "Mechanics and Workingmen" of the city and county of Philadelphia, at which the workingmen decided "to take the management of their own interests as a class, into their own immediate keeping ... and to support such men only for the City Councils and State Legislature, as shall pledge themselves in their official capacity to support the interests and claims of the working classes."[122]

Before we describe the steps which led to the formation of the new political movement in Philadelphia, it is necessary to describe briefly the electoral system of the Jacksonian era. Candidates for public office were nominated by convention and caucus meetings which were usually tightly controlled by machine politicians. Party membership involved only the loosest sort of attachment; there was no device for registration, as is the custom today. Property qualifications were general for all office holders, thus placing limits on those who might be nominated. Methods of voting were crude. At polling stations, voters were handed printed ballots (usually distinctively colored and shaped) by politicians from contending parties. Secrecy, under such circumstances, was virtually nonexistent. Corruption was common and violence frequent, due to the bitterness with which machine politicians fought for petty graft.[123]

Late in May 1828, the Mechanics' Union of Trade Associations authorized its recording secretary to open the organization's political campaign officially by placing a resolution and preamble in the *Mechanics' Free Press*. The resolution requested the delegates to "lay the subject before the several trade societies and report severally at our stated meeting (in July) on the expediency of adopting measures for nominating suitable persons to represent the interests of the working classes in the city councils and state legislature." Heighton, who had written the resolution, gave it ample space in the labor paper, and called upon the workingmen to "drive these money changers from the temple of freedom, and restore its furtive purity, the legacy of our fathers."[124] The cordwainers, hatters, and carpenters, the chief unions in the Mechanics' Union, responded quickly. The carpenters resolved unanimously that "we entertain the most heartfelt satisfaction and approbation for the measures in contemplation by the said *Mechanics' Union of Trade Associations*, and will use every exertion to carry the said measures in effect."[125]

The year 1828 was the year of the presidential election between the incumbent John Quincy Adams, running for reelection, and General Andrew Jackson. But the Mechanics' Union had decided to avoid the presidential election entirely, "The feeling," Louis H. Arky notes, "was that national politics was fraught with highhandedness and workingmen could not cope with problems of such wide scope."[126] Further to avoid this danger, the Association did not refer to its political venture as a party. But this fooled no one, and its action was treated in the contemporary press as introducing a new party into the political arena of Philadelphia—the Working Men's Party. The new Party would join the two existing political organizations, the Federalist Party, which still flourished in Philadelphia although it was extinguished elsewhere in the nation, and the Democratic Party. The latter was split into two factions, the Administration or Adams Party, and the Jackson Party. In 1828, before the elections, the Federalist Party was in control, but the Jackson Party was coming up strongly.[127]

The fall elections for City Council offices and State legislative posts thus became the points at which the Working Men's Party would concentrate all of its attention.[128] The *Mechanics' Free Press* was its organ, and in it Heighton prodded the workers to nominate and elect candidates of their own choosing for these positions.[129]

During August, the month of political conventions, the Mechanics' Union of Trade Associations called three meetings to discuss the "propriety of nominating suitable persons to be supported at the ensuing elections." The meetings were to be held in the city and county, the first in the District Court room in the city; the second in the Northern Liberties, to the northeast of the city, and the third at the Commissioner's Hall, Southwark, the most densely populated district in the county. Heighton, who considered the meetings crucial to the future of the movement, called upon all workingmen to attend and to urge their shopmates to join them. After the meetings, he reported angrily that an attempt had been "made by certain lawyers and speculators, to distract the meetings...."[130]

This was an understatement. Two of the meetings were dominated by "unparliamentary brawls." The first, in the city's District Court room, proceeded without interruption, but at the Commissioner's Hall in Southwark, an unruly mob, mainly Jackson men, repeatedly denounced Michael Labarthe, a hatter, who was the chairman, of being "an Adams' man," and called for the audience to "throw the chairman out of the window...." Only with great difficulty could Labarthe secure passage of the resolutions supporting the stand of the Mechanics' Union of Trade Associations, and to appoint committees to attend the nominating convention of the whole county.[131]

At the Southwark meeting an effort was also made to adopt three preambles and constitutions. But the speakers were drowned out in the melee, and the meeting had to be adjourned. However Heighton, secretary of the meeting, recalled the disbanded assembly, and delivered a prepared speech which was published later under the title *The Principles of Aristocratic Legislation, developed in an Address to the Working People of the district of Southwark, and townships of Moyanmensing and Passyunk, in the Commissioner's Hall, August 14, 1828, By an Operative Citizen.*[132] The third of Heighton's three anonymous pamphlets, it advanced a number of the same ideas he had previously enunciated. But here he put a new emphasis on the fact that working men were carrying the full tax burden in the community although they were not property owners, and had only their own labor to offer. As a result, they were forced to pay rent over and over again, many times the true value of the wretched buildings they occupied, and far more than the owners of the properties paid in taxes. Their rent, moreover, not only amortized the original investment and the land and building improvements, but even supported the various "public improvements" under construction. But in the working-class areas, streets were in poor repair, rubbish was never washed away, and water pumps had not been erected.[133]

Out of the district meetings organized in response to the call from the Mechanics' Union of Trade Associations came nominating conventions where popularly elected delegates chose candidates for city and state offices. In the name of the Working Men's Ticket, candidates were entered for all 39 municipal and county offices, but none for any of the three congressional seats. Only 8 of the candidates endorsed were exclusively on the Working Men's ticket, the remaining being chosen either from the Administration (Adams) or Jackson choices. Delegations of workingmen visited each of the major party candidates, inquiring if he would support the workingmen's program if elected, "thus drawing attention to the politicians that another block of voters was at hand whose interests had to be noted."[134]

Of the exclusively workingmen's candidates, only two had been previously mentioned as being involved in labor activities. They were James Glasgow, plasterer, who ran for common council, and James McAllister, shoemaker, candidate for City Assembly. In general, the Working Men's Party had no objection to supporting candidates of whatever social background or political persuasion—so long as they pledged to support the workingmen's program. But the *Mechanics' Free Press*, the Party's official organ, expressed the fear that the Democratic Party represented the main danger to the new political movement, "for as most of us are deserters from their ranks, they view us with the same sensation as the mighty lord would the revolt of his vassals; there cannot be so much danger from the Federalists, for generally speaking we were never inclined to trust them."[135]

Heighton, who voiced this fear, was deeply bothered by the fact that the workingmen had nominated candidates who, while worthy were still not "in *entire* accordance with the recently developed political principles." Perhaps that is why he praised the Working Men's ticket lukewarmly, characterizing it as being "in many respects unobjectionable."[136]

The Federalists and the Democrats had not ignored the appearance of the Working Men's Party. On the contrary, they sought both to confuse the workingmen and win their votes by attaching to themselves the air of being the real spokespersons for the workingmen. The press reported that electioneering carriages carried signs reading "The Working Men's Ticket coupled with the names of Jackson and Adams."[137]

All of this, Heighton was convinced, coming on top of the fact that the entire city was engulfed in the presidential campaign, guaranteed that the workingmen's candidates would not score a large vote. He assured his readers, however, that it was "of trifling importance, whether the efforts of the Working People of this year become successful, or the contrary," so long as the foundation of a PEOPLE'S party was laid, "based upon the immutable rock of *equality*, industry, utility, and the real intelligence of mankind."[138]

The national triumph of Andrew Jackson in 1828 was also repeated in the presidential and local elections in Philadelphia. Jackson swept the city, and all three Jackson congressional candidates won easily. In the city election, the Jackson Democrats averaged 4,500 votes to about 3,500 for the Adamsites, while three of the exclusively workingmen's candidates polled about 240 votes each, and another received 539. In the county, four exclusively workingmen's candidates received about 420 votes; however, William O. Kline, a lawyer selected by the Working Men's Party at the last moment (although he was a regular Jackson Democrat) received the high vote of 1,400.[139] The Jacksonians did nominate three candidates for the City Assembly and twelve for the Common Council who were also on the Working Men's Ticket. But this could not obscure the fact that votes for the candidates of the Working Men's Party, when they ran alone, ranged from 240 to 539.[140]

The Workingmen's Party thus emerged from its first electoral contest in October 1828 with an unpromising future. Of its 39 candidates for state and national legislatures, only those who ran as joint candidates on other tickets were elected. Those who ran alone on the Workingmen's Party ticket received less than one-tenth the vote of their Democratic rivals.[141]

Heighton explained this poor showing as the inevitable birth pangs of a new political party and, in part, he was correct.[142] But a more important cause was undoubtedly the popularity of Andrew Jackson, who carried Philadelphia by a large plurality.[143] In 1828 many Philadelphia workingmen were hopeful that the election of Jackson and his fellow Democrats would herald a new era of justice for American producers. In Jackson, widely touted as the candidate of the producing classes and not merely as a spokesperson for the frontiersmen,[144] they saw a means to end the exploitation of the producing classes. But by the summer of 1829, as Jackson finished making his federal appointments, even the smallest of such hopes were dashed. Ignoring his closest counselors, "Old Hickory" appointed conservative party men to the most important Pennsylvania posts and ignored his earliest and most ardent supporters. Among those passed over was William John Duane, whom Jackson had originally intended to appoint as the federal district attorney for eastern Pennsylvania in recognition of his liberalism and his father's early support of his candidacy. Disgusted by Jackson's appointments and his betrayal of the workingman, working-class Philadelphia viewed the Workingmen's Party as the logical choice for the 1829 elections.[145]

Undaunted by the poor showing in the first attempt, the Working Men's Party of Philadelphia immediately made plans for the next election. Heighton was convinced that this time, with the interest in the presidential race no longer dominating the political scene, the outcome would be different. The first attempt had been "unsuccessful," he assured the workingmen, "owing to circumstances which are temporary in nature." New circumstances would bring different results.[146]

The bitter winter of 1829, causing incredible suffering among the laboring classes of Philadelphia, strengthened Heighton's confidence. Unemployment was general, and this along with the low wages of those lucky enough to have work "made it difficult for even the penurious to meet the rising cost of living."[147] Wood, which had sold in the early fall of 1828 at $5.50 a cord, now sold at from $8.00 to $10.00 a cord.[148] Matthew Carey commented:

Thousands of our labouring people travel hundreds of miles in quest of employment on canals, at 62, 75, and 87 cents per day, paying a dollar and a half or two dollars a week for their board, leaving families behind; depending on them for support. They labour frequently in marshy grounds which destroys their health, often irrevocably. They return to their poor families—with ruined constitutions, with a sorry pittance, most labouriously earned, and take to their beds sick and unable to work. Hundreds are swept off annually, many of them leaving numerous and helpless families. Notwithstanding their wretched fate, their places are quickly supplied by others, although death stares them in the face.[149]

In 1829 a committee of 90 prominent Philadelphia women and 138 men sent a petition to the War Department protesting the pay received by women home workers making shirts for the army. An expert seamstress, they said, by working from morning to night could make no more than fifty cents a day. Moreover, they were frequently out of work. The War Department replied that it could do nothing, since the issue was "so intimately connected with the manufacturing interests and the general prices of this kind of labor in the city of Philadelphia."[150]

All over Philadelphia expert seamstresses working early and late could make no more than $1.12 1/2 cents per week from which fifty cents was deducted for lodging, "leaving 62 1/2 cents per week or nine cents a day for food and other necessities of life."[151]

William Heighton was confident that the burgeoning discontent in Philadelphia's labor circles would find expression in support of the Working Men's Party. But he also realized that the Mechanics' Union of Trade Associations, while having performed a valuable service in developing the movement, could not serve as an effective vehicle for the Party, "since it restricted itself only to artisans in the trade." It was necessary to attract the workingmen outside the skilled crafts, and for this a different type of organization had to be created.[152]

In the election of 1828 the new party had relied upon "Committees of Vigilance" set up by county nominating conventions. As early as November 1828, barely a month after the election, Heighton urged that "ward political clubs" be established, and he advised the workers to "go to the assessors" and "have themselves duly assessed" in order to be "eligible to the right of Franchise." The clubs would serve several purposes. They would assist in the main object of electing "our own public officers," and would, also establish a fund which would enable clubs to perform a variety of services. These would include the "general diffusion of constitutional, legal and political knowledge among the working peoples." By printing legislative enactments and information on important legislation, members would become better acquainted with their contents. The clubs would also encourage debates on the merits of current issues, thereby aiding in the formation of intelligent opinion among workers. They would furnish free legal advice to their members. Finally, they would require all candidates of the Working Men's Party, following their elections to use "their influence in procurement of appropriations of public money" for legislative demands put forward by the workingmen.[153]

In November 1828, Southwark took the lead in forming the first "Republican Political Association of Working Men." Other districts and wards followed, each one calling itself by the same name. In announcing its formation, the Southwark Association declared that its purpose was "to check ... that glaring aristocracy and political intrigue, which has so long preyed on the vitals of our republic, and doomed to slavery so large and useful a portion of our fellow men."[154]

In March 1829 the Republican Political Association of the Working Men of the City of Philadelphia was formed. It began at once to organize the workingmen for the fall elections of 1829. Nominations for office were left to the city and county conventions. Delegates were chosen democratically at ward meetings to attend city and county nominating conventions. In an effort to avoid commitments to either of the old parties, and in response to the warnings of many ward meetings against fusion with the Federalists or Democrats, the nominating conventions selected candidates before the other parties met. Even so, the Federalists endorsed nine and the Democrats three of the Working Men's candidates for city offices, and the former also endorsed three assembly and senate candidates.[155]

As the Working Men's Party organized itself into an effective political force, the opposition press seized upon the visits of Frances Wright to Philadelphia in the summer and fall of 1829 as a means of discrediting the movement. The young Scottish woman who lectured in the United States in behalf of free oppor-

tunities for women and the rights of labor, had become con-
verted to the Utopian Socialism of Robert Owen, and had become a vigorous advocate of an educational plan which was
soon called "state guardianship." The proponents of the plan insisted that children should be instructed in communities where
they would live from early childhood. In the state boarding
schools, they would wear the same clothing, experience the same
treatment, and be taught in the same branches of learning. There-
would be no room for religious instruction; only knowledge
based on practical, realistic experience would be in the curriculum, and all clerical influence in education would be eliminated.[156]

During the election campaign of 1829, Frances Wright delivered two speeches in Philadelphia. In the first, "A Lecture on
Existing Evils and Their Remedy," at the Arch Street Theatre on
June 2, she spelled out in detail her "state guardianship" plan of
education.[157] Wright's educational principles, and the presence
on the platform at the Arch Street Theatre of Abner Kneeland,
the controversial pastor who was accused of heresy, made her
appearance in the city an issue in the election of 1829.[158] William
Heighton did not endorse Wright's address, even though notice
of her speeches were widely advertised in the Mechanics' Free
Press, and the trade unions and workingmen's ward clubs made
it clear that they had nothing to do with any attacks on religion.
But the opposition press tried hard to tie the militant female
lecturer to the Working Men's program. In 1829, however, this
effort was not effective. On the contrary, as one contemporary
noted, the attacks, "by their unjust calumny, induced hundreds
to go and listen to her lectures."[159]

The results of the 1829 election were dramatically different
from those of the previous year. In 1829, 16 Working Men's Party
candidates were elected, as were all but one of those who ran on
multi-party tickets. In all, the Party polled close to 2,400 votes in
the city and county, nearly three times the number received the
year before. Heighton was jubilant. "The balance of power has at
length got into the hands of the working people, where it properly belongs," he declared, "and it will be used, in the future for
the general weal."[160] Although he was wrong about his prediction, his assessment of the local political situation was accurate.
In 1829, the Working Men's Party did hold the balance of power

in Philadelphia, a fact attested to by the serious efforts of the Democratic Party to win working-class votes and to include working-class candidates on their city tickets. A month later, in November 1829, the Mechanics' Union of Trade Associations, which had started the political movement of Philadelphia workingmen, disbanded.[161] The Working Men's Party of Philadelphia, however, survived the demise of its founder.

In September 1829, Heighton delivered three addresses on "The Rights of the Working People and the Cause of Universal Education." Unfortunately, the speeches were never published.[162] But the basic principles and ideas of the speeches were published in the "Report of the Working Men's Committee on Public Education," written by Heighton.

In September 1829, the Working Men's Republican Political Associations of Southwark, the Northern Liberties, and the City each appointed education subcommittees "to ascertain the state of public instruction in Pennsylvania, and to digest and propose such improvements in education as may be deemed essential to the intellectual and moral prosperity of the people." The three committees met several times that fall to cooperate in their efforts, and assigned William Heighton to prepare their report. At three meetings of the "friends of general and equal education," on February 4, 8, and 11, 1830, the joint committee's report, written by Heighton, was read, discussed, and unanimously adopted, along with two bills to be submitted to the legislature.[163]

The report was widely copied and reprinted in the labor press and later printed in pamphlet form for general distribution. It begins by stating that, as a result of their investigations, the committees were "forced into the conviction, that there is great defect in the educational system of Pennsylvania; and that much remains to be accomplished before it will have reached that point of improvement which the resources of the state would justify, and which the intellectual condition of the people and the preservation of our republican institutions demand." The plain fact of the matter was that, with the exception of Philadelphia, Lancaster, and Pittsburgh (which had been organized into school districts since 1818), the "entire state [was] destitute of any provisions for public instruction" other than that minimal support provided by the School Act of 1809. This law called for each county to report to the state the number of school-age children residing there whose parents could not afford to educate them. It permitted these children to be "instructed at the most convenient schools" at county expense, but made no provision to ascertain the accuracy of the head counts, to oversee the quality of the schools receiving funds, or to guarantee that each child would, in fact, be educated.

The 1809 law was often flouted and ignored, the report declared. Its provisions were so general and incomplete that they were "frequently inoperative"; they were, "in some instances but partially executed; in others, perverted and abused—and in many cases entirely and culpably neglected." The committees had received reports of embezzlement of funds by county assessors, of failures to report the true number of children in need of educational assistance, and of the "illegal and intentional exclusion" of some children from the educational benefits called for in the law. Too often, the report noted, "from a parsimonious desire of saving the county funds, the cheapest, and consequently the most inefficient schools have been usually selected by the commissioners of the several counties."

While the schools in Philadelphia, Lancaster, and Pittsburgh were immeasurably better than those in other parts of the state, the report emphasized that even in these districts, the situation was in need of vast improvement. The principle problem was that "their leading feature is pauperism!" By being "confined exclusively to the children of the poor," the schools in these districts effectively closed out large numbers of children. The report declared that there were probably "thousands of children whose parents [were] unable to afford them a good private education, yet whose standing, professions or connections in society effectually exclude them from taking the benefit of a poor law." The stigma of charity worked against even "those poorest parents" whose children qualified for free schooling under the law. In spite of the avowed philanthropy of charity schools, pride and a sense of self-worth stood in the way of these schools effectively reaching even those for whom they were intended. There were "great numbers" of parents who believed that "a dependence on the public bounty [was] incompatible with the rights and liberties of an American citizen, and whose deep and cherished consciousness of independence determine[d] them rather to starve the intellect of their offspring, than to submit to become the objects of public charity." Even those parents who might be willing to swallow their pride were often unable to send their children to school, for many were so poor as to be "totally unable to maintain and clothe their children, while at the schools." These children received no schooling and were forced, by their parents' extreme poverty, into child labor or an early apprenticeship.

The report was also sharply critical of the curriculum and instruction received by "the comparatively small number of youth who enjoy (the) benefits" of the public school system. The instruction extended "in no case further than a tolerable proficiency in reading, writing, and arithmetic, and sometimes to a slight acquaintance with geography. Besides these, the girls are taught a few simple branches of industry." These paltry offerings constituted a "radical and glaring defect" in the existing schools and in no way would fulfill the real aims of education, which should be "the production of a just disposition, virtuous habits, and a rational self-governing character."

The report was also concerned about the lack of any provision for the care and instruction of children under five years of age. This situation created hardship for working parents, who were "compelled to keep [their] elder children from the school to take charge of the younger ones." The report indicated that the damage thus done was twofold: the older children were deprived of an education and the infants were subjected to "pernicious influences and impressions at an early age" as their untutored siblings "scattered the seeds of vice over the infant soil."

Finally, the report blasted the overseers of the school fund for class bias in their allocations. While a "very large proportion of youth (were) either partially or entirely destitute of education," the state had supported colleges and universities with "liberal supplies from the public purse." This constituted an appropriation "exclusively for the benefit of the wealthy, who (were) thereby enabled to procure a liberal education for their children, upon lower terms than it could otherwise be afforded them." Though not opposed to higher education, the report warned that this practice, if continued, would "serve to engender an aristocracy of talent and place knowledge, the chief element of power, in the hands of the privileged few." Such a "monopoly of talent," the "original element of despotism," was clearly dangerous to the "healthy existence of a free government," as it "consigns the multitude to comparative ignorance, and secures the balance of knowledge on the side of the rich and the rulers." The report closed with the observation that "this monopoly should be broken up, and ... the means of equal knowledge, (the only security for equal liberty) should be rendered, by legal provision, the common property of all classes."[164]

William Heighton's criticisms of the existing state of educational arrangements were directed specifically at Pennsylvania. But the same general complaints were echoed by workers all over the country, and Heighton's report became a valuable weapon in labor's struggle for a universal system of public education.[165]

Meanwhile, the workingmen's political movement in Philadelphia, one of whose key objectives was to achieve the type of educational system envisaged in Heighton's report, became active again. Encouraged by the success in 1829, the Working Men's Party eagerly made preparations for the next year's campaign. Meetings were held, and there was a determined effort to build an even more efficient organization in the city and county to get out the labor vote. In Southwark the local Working Men's Republican Political Association issued an address to its membership and supporters, urging them to "prepare for the coming season." Throughout the spring of 1830, organization advanced. To the city convention of 1830 delegates came from fifteen wards.[166]

But at the same time that the Party was spreading and consolidating its influence, it was being infiltrated by political opportunists, and weakened by both internal dissension and by new attacks from without. In the spring of 1830, Heighton issued a new warning of the dangers that faced the movement:

> That our enemies are making use of every possible stratagem to effect a disunion in our ranks, is too well known; they have shown this cloven foot in many instances; and without our real friends watch them closely, they will succeed in effecting their object. It would be well for our friends in this city, and in all parts of the Union, to be firm to their purpose; their principles are worth contending for and must eventually succeed....[167]

Unfortunately, Heighton himself contributed to the internal conflict. During the 1830 campaign the question of candidates for public office was widely discussed: should only workingmen be nominated for office or should "tried friends" of the movement be nominated as well? It would seem from the resolutions of the ward clubs and county conventions that a majority favored the nomination of both workingmen and "tried friends" of the movement, but insisted that the latter be truly devoted to the working class and not include employers, lawyers, and rich men eager only to secure workingmen's votes to advance their political careers. But Heighton insisted that anyone who pledged to support the workingmen's program should be nominated and supported for election, and this included employers:

> If an employer superintends his own business (still more if he works with his own hands) he is a working man.... If the view of this be correct, shall we look with a jealous eye on those employers who prefer being considered working men? Who are willing to join us in obtaining our objects?[168]

It certainly did not sit well with many Philadelphia workingmen that the leading spokesperson for the Working Men's Party was willing to countenance employers playing important roles in the movement—so long as they were willing to join in "obtaining our objects."[169]

The issue also emerged sharply over the Congressional candidate chosen by the Working Men's Party. In 1830, the Party entered the congressional elections for the first time, nominating Stephen Simpson from the first district. Born in Philadelphia of fairly well-to-do parents, Simpson attracted attention in radical circles with the publication in 1831 of *The Workingmen's Manual: A New Theory of Political Economy of the Principle of Production as the Source of Wealth*. An early worshipper of General Andrew Jackson, whom he had fought under in the Battle of New Orleans, he turned against his idol when he failed to obtain a position in the new Administration. He shifted his attention to the young Working Men's Party; and embraced a radical social program. But this did not prevent the Federalist Party from nominating Simpson for Congress from the first Congressional district, a fact which did not keep the Working Men's Party from naming him as a candidate for the same position.[170]

While Heighton rejoiced over Simpson's choice, many workingmen viewed him as an opportunist who moved in and out of causes to advance his own career, Nor did the fact that his answers to the questions submitted by the Working Men's Party's nominating committee showed him to be a champion of the working class and a critic of the exploitation of capital by labor, entirely diminish this feeling. In his answer, Simpson opposed paper currency, "oppressive taxation," imprisonment for debt, the militia system, and championed a democratic public education system.[171]

In addition to internal discord, the Working Men's Party faced a well-organized attack from the commercial newspapers during the 1830 campaign. Charges of "anti-religion," "infidelity," "agrarianism," and "workeyism" were hurled at the movement. Although Frances Wright made no appearance in Philadelphia in this campaign, her previous visits were recalled, and since she was increasingly under attack in nearby New York City for her religious and educational views, she was now credited by the Philadelphia press with being the ideological parent of the workingmen's movement. The Working Men's Party answered that it had no sympathy with the agrarians, was not connected with Frances Wright, and stated that "those who introduce either the subject of Agrarianism or religion into our political proceedings are the avowed enemies of our righteous cause."[172]

But the campaign, coming on top of the internal discord, had its effect. The Working Men's Party did increase its average by about 300; its candidates received from 812 to 1,047 votes, and all eight of those also nominated by the Democrats were victorious. In the Northern Liberties, eight labor candidates were elected as county commissioners. Nevertheless, the Party lost the balance of power it had held in 1829, and prospects did not appear bright that it would ever regain it.[173]

The election returns in 1830 came as a bitter blow to William Heighton, and for the first time the editor of the *Mechanics' Free Press* and the inspirer of independent working class political action expressed real discouragement. The poor showing was no longer the result of enemy maneuvers; the workers themselves were to blame this time. "The election of 1830," he wrote bitterly, "adds another instance of the blindness of the workingmen to their interests and exhibits in bold and striking color how easily the public liberties may be endangered by the sappiness of the people themselves."[174]

But "A Working Man" reminded Heighton that the character of the candidates nominated by the Working Men's Party had failed to arouse enthusiasm among the workingmen of Philadelphia, and he questioned the wisdom of "selecting men ... whose interests are to great bank charters and all kinds of monopolies." The last was a reference to the fact that during the election, two of the men nominated on the Working Men's Ticket had turned out to be agents of the monopolists, and had been forced on the Ticket "against the manifest desire of the majority of the Delegates." The lesson was that "no man can serve two masters," but it was a lesson some of the leaders of the Working Men's Party had forgotten.

Nothing, however, could lift Heighton's depressed spirits. Shortly after the election of 1830, he left Philadelphia a disillusioned man. He never returned. Nor is there any record that he ever again participated in the labor movement.[175]

Heighton emerged only once after he left Philadelphia. In 1865 he came out in favor of Radical Reconstruction, urging that in addition to legal freedom under the Thirteenth Amendment, the former slaves had to gain civil and economic freedom.[176]

A few months after Heighton left Philadelphia, the Working Men's Party disappeared from the scene. They nominated candidates for the various city posts in the spring 1831 campaign, but did worse than before, failing to elect any candidates.[177] It was the last campaign for the first labor party in the world.

Describing the Philadelphia labor movement in the Jacksonian era, A. Fuller Spaulding wrote of a subculture manifested

> in the radical and rationalist debating clubs, lyceums, and discussion groups, where Tom Paine's progeny brought its critical inquiry of the Enlightenment to bear on the emerging question of class. Apparently rooted in a stratum of native-born American artisans, the radicals were avid readers, patronized the Society of Free Inquirers and the Universalist Church, defended the labour theory of value and other tenets of classical political economy, and found their most effective spokesman in William Heighton. This English-born workingclass activist and intellectual was a shoemaker who shifted radicalism from a purely political focus towards an understanding of the unity of political and economic life; he had the strongest appeal among the most literate mechanics.[178]

By the time he left Philadelphia, William Heighton had become well known in the contemporary labor movement under the unassuming pseudonym of "An Unlettered Mechanic." He had achieved a secure (if neglected) place in the history of the American labor movement. He had invigorated the Philadelphia labor movement with a series of addresses which were also printed as pamphlets and which, when distributed along the Eastern seaboard, helped invigorate the labor movements in New York, Boston and other cities. He had popularized the socialist labor theory of value, and had contributed immensely to breaking down allegiance limited to particular crafts and replacing it with an all-craft solidarity. He had initiated the first organization through which the mechanics could act as a unit—the Mechanics' Union of Trade Associations. He had helped establish the first Mechanics' Free Library, the first labor paper the United States, the *Mechanics' Free Press*, and the first labor party ever established—the Working Men's Party of Philadelphia. While these and other aspects of the Philadelphia workingmen's movement of the Jacksonian era owe much to the writings and efforts of Robert Owen and the English Ricardian Socialists, they owed their existence mainly to William Heighton.

In his pamphlets, speeches, editorials in the *Mechanics' Free Press*, reports, and resolutions he prepared for the workingmen's movement of Philadelphia, Heighton advanced the cause of progressive reform directed towards correcting the faults of existing society and advancing the cause of social and economic equality. Among the demands he championed were those for a mechanics' lien law, for the abolition of imprisonment for debt, for a less expensive legal system, for equal taxation, for all officers to be elected by the people, for the abolition of the existing militia system, for the abolition of chartered monopolies, and for free, universal, public education. He played a crucial role in organizing the first mass-based, popular movement for democratic public schools. The paper he edited discussed the education question in almost every issue, and Heighton, in his editorials and other writings, popularized many of the most important arguments in favor of equal, universal, public education. He proclaimed the right of workers to an education as citizens of the republic; that education had to be equal for all, with no class distinction, and that it should be made universally available to every school-age child. He exposed the class bias in education and rejected the charity school concept as an appropriate form of working class education. He was totally committed to the position that schools should be tax-supported and under the control of a popular government.

The workingmen's political movement that Heighton, more than any other labor figure of the period, helped bring into being, though unsuccessful in electing many candidates, created alarm among the major parties. They moved quickly to demoralize and divide the movement. At the same time, they proclaimed their support of the workingmen's measures. "Many of the reforms called for by the workingmen," declared the *Working Man's Advocate* in 1830, "are now acknowledged to be just and reasonable, and are even advocated by several of presses which have hitherto supported the party in power...."[179] There have been very little real movement on any of these "reforms" until the rise of the Working Men's Party. Soon afterwards, many politicians of both parties began to sense the popular support for these "reforms."

In the spring of 1831, a few months after William Heighton left Philadelphia in despair, the *Mechanics' Free Press* reported: "We are happy to find that the lien law was passed which gives to mechanics, journeymen and labourers a security for the labour expended in improving our cities, and adding to the comforts of their inhabitants."[180] In June 1833, the Pennsylvania state legislature approved "an act to abolish imprisonment for debt and other purposes." A year later the legislature finally passed the law establishing a comprehensive structure of free public schools. Under the act of 1834, if the majority of the citizens authorized it, tax was to be levied to support common schools.[181]

William A. Sullivan concludes his study of the Working Men's Party of Philadelphia with the observation: "labor had won." Its program had been incorporated into the platform of the two major parties, and its major demands had been enacted into legislation.[182]

II. Selections From William Heighton's Writings and Speeches

Extract from *An Address to the Members of Trade Societies and to the Working Classes Generally**

The last class which comes under our notice is that of Legislators. These constitute in point of intelligence and influence the most powerful class of men in the nation. They are elected *by the great body of the people* as THEIR REPRESENTATIVES, and invested with powers which enable them to make such general and particular *social arrangements* as in their judgment are best calculated to supply the wants to provide for the necessities, and in every way to promote the just interests, EQUALLY, of each individual among the whole body of their constituents. The therefore have duties to perform, above all others the most important. It is their business to support and regulate, and if necessary, with the approbation of their constituents, to *create* such national institutions as are best calculated to promote, equally, the happiness and prosperity of ALL the people. They frame our national and state laws, and through these they rule not only our *collective*, but also to an indefinite and unlimited extent, our *individual* destinies. It is therefore their supreme duty so to legislate, that not only our national prosperity shall be continually advancing; but also that *the individual member of the community, may improve in exact proportion as the national prosperity itself increases.*

Now the question which naturally comes before us is this, *have they so legislated?* Do we find now, while the number of useful,

---

* *An Address to the Members of Trade Societies and to the Working Classes Generally, Being an Exposition of Relative Situation, Condition, and Future Prospects of Working People of the United States of America, Together with a Suggestion and Outlines of a Plan by which they may gradually and indefinitely improve their condition.* By a Fellow-Labourer, Philadelphia, Published by the Author, 1827.

labour-saving inventions is every day increasing, and arts and manufactures rapidly improving; while our national facilities for the creation of wealth are such, that our markets are every where beginning to be gutted!! While articles of wealth of every description, whether of food, clothing, furniture, or any other articles of necessity or convenience are so abundant in our stores, that the vendors of them know not how nor where to dispose to them!! While the incessant industry and toils of the working class, have created in the nation such a superabundance of wealth, I ask, do we find our labours beginning to be abridged or lessened? Do we find that instead of having to labour as formerly from ten to fourteen hours per day to obtain moderate conveniences, we can now obtain many of the luxuries of life with the labour of five or six?

Surely we, the working class, who constitute a vast majority of the nation, and as such possess an interest which ought, in the estimation of our legislators, to be reckoned at least *equal* in point of importance with the interest of any other class in the nation; we who create all the wealth that is created, and by the proceeds of whose labour *they* are exclusively maintained and supported; we the great mass of the people, who by our sovereign voice raise them to the stations which they fill, for the express purpose of promoting our interests, intelligence, and happiness; surely I say, we have a right to expect, that in our present state of increasing national prosperity, such an improvement in our *individual* condition will be the natural result of their legislative proceedings.

Since the introduction into common use of scientific inventions and improvements, has enabled a given quantity of manual labour to produce fifty, and in some instances perhaps an hundred fold more of wealth than the same labour would have produced previous to their introduction; and since in consequence of them, all the markets in the world are becoming crammed to overflowing with wealth of every description, insomuch that the demand for productive labor is rapidly decreasing, and productive employment growing every day more difficult to be obtained, we have a right to expect, from these OUR REPRESENTATIVES, the establishment of such legislative regulations; or if these are not sufficient, of such NEW INSTITUTIONS as will enable us to retain in our own hands a due and equitable proportion of the products of our own labour; and instead of our having to labour as at present from ten to sixteen hours per day for a *mere subsistence,* that, in exact proportion as scientific improvements and inventions *increase*, our labour may in the same proportion be *diminished* from twelve to ten hours per day, and from that down to eight, to six, and so on, until the development and progress of science has reduced human labour to its lowest term. If it be indeed the duty of legislators to promote the interests and happiness (not of a few only) but of *the great mass* of their constituents, then surely there can be no object of legislation which ought to claim so much of their consideration as this. But mark! how great the difference. It is a fact which cannot be too often brought to view, that the more the national prosperity increases through our labours, the more difficult do we find it to obtain the means of subsistence; and the sooner do we, the producers of it, sink into a state of degradation and poverty!!

I think this fact is now too clear to admit of refutation, and proves beyond a doubt that legislators do abuse, and grossly too, that power which is placed in their hands for the sole purpose of promoting THE PUBLIC GOOD. They encourage the invention and use of machinery under the influence of commercial *competition*, a principle which renders it a curse instead of a blessing to the great mass of their constituents. If commercial competition is *necessarily unavoidable*, and *cannot* be dispensed with or abolished, why encourage invention; seeing it is only calculated to advance the interests of a few, while it places the great body of the people, that is the working classes, in a state of hopeless poverty? Why not rather *inflict penalties* than grant patent rights to the inventors of machinery? If they foresee the miseries which soon or late it must bring upon society, where is their *honesty* in sacrificing the happiness of the greatest portion of their constituents to the avaricious desires of a few overgrown capitalists? And if on the other hand they do not foresee them, then where is that *intelligence* which should fit them to become the *leaders* of the people? Can men, who suffer a subject of such immense importance to their constituents to pass by them unobserved, until the error is seen by individuals whose thinking faculties are in the great measure restrained by incessant application to physical labour; men, who lag behind the lowest class of the people in the glorious march of human improvement, can these, I say be worthy of being called *their leaders?*

This supine negligence on the part of men, whom we have a right to look up to as guides to a state of general and *individual* prosperity and happiness, can (I think) only be accounted for upon one principle, and that I shall endeavour to explain.

The fact is this, the class of men we are now considering under the name of Legislators, are in themselves, so far as relates to the production of wealth, as helpless as infants; unable to create by their own labour the most common necessaries of life. They are *consumers only*, producing nothing, and as such dependent on our exertions for all the wealth they possess or enjoy. Rents, interest on money, profit on labour and salaries, are the principal sources by which they accumulate the wealth which is created by the working class; they therefore have a DIRECT INTEREST in supporting these institutions a legal but unjust abstraction. And be assured, that so long as we choose men to be our legislators, who subsist and accumulate *through these sources*, they will ever consider it their *interest* to keep us in a state of continual toil and poverty; that they may thereby reap the benefit of our labours, and revel in a splendour of wealth which arises out of our degradation!

Was ever a class of men heard of, who acted in direct opposition to what they conceived to be THEIR INTERESTS? No never. The past experience of the world sufficiently proves that legislators (as a class of men) have never promoted the interest of their constituents any farther than as those constituents have possessed an interest *in unison with their own*, and have directed them by the voice of public opinion communicated through the medium of the PRESS. Now the direction which legislators have hitherto received, has invariably been given by individuals, who, like themselves, accumulate wealth without producing it, and *therefore* have an interest in accordance with their own, and opposed to the interests of the working class; as for instance, by those who are occupied in commercial pursuits; by individuals of the independent class; by judges, counsellors, lawyers, theologians, &c. It is among these only, that those are to be found who write for the instruction of legislators, and of course the public opinion expressed by them, can be favourable only to their interests.

On the other hand the working class have NO individual interests, in unison with those of their legislators. They live upon that small portion of the products of their labour which is left to them after the all devouring taxes of rent, usury, profit and salaries have been levied upon it; or in other words, after the non-productive classes—through these means—have reveled upon and consumed the choicest products of it. It is true, in this favored nation we enjoy the inestimable blessing of "universal suffrage," and constituting as we every where do, a very great majority, *we have the power* to choose our own legislators. But let it be recollected, this blessing, (like invention) however great *in itself* can be of no further benefit to us, than as we possess sufficient *knowledge* to make a proper use of it. IT WILL BE an instrument of unlimited good to the great mass of the people when they shall possess that degree of intelligence which will enable them to direct it *for their own benefit*; but at present this very blessing is suffered, through our want of information, to be directed against our prosperity and welfare by individuals whose interest is at variance with ours. I mean by those who *nominate* candidates for legislative offices. These persons invariably belong to the non-productive classes; and of course invariably nominate candidates, whose *interests* are in accordance with their own. Thus the *first choice* which is that of *nominating*, is always assumed by the useless and accumulating classes, who constitute but a small minority of the people; and after that the *second choice* (election) is but a mere matter of form, for if we, the working class should have a choice, out of twenty different candidates for one office, we should not find an individual among them all, who would be found faithfully to represent *our interests*, for the simple reason above explained, that the interests of *such nominated* candidates, are universally at variance with and conflicting against ours. And as to the influence of *public opinion*, on the proceeding of legislators; although next to that of *interest*, it is perhaps the most powerful motive to proper conduct that we have any knowledge of; yet it is a fact too well known for me to dwell on, that we as a class have never yet acquired sufficient intelligence to possess such an opinion; and if we did, it is doubtful whether there are at present any facilities existing, through which the expression of it would be allowed to reach our legislative assemblies.

I think it is pretty clear from what has been said concerning this class, that we shall never reap any benefit from their official proceedings until we have men of our own *nominating*, men *whose interests are in unison with ours*; and a public opinion of our own by which in some measure to direct and regulate their proceedings.

Let us suppose for a moment, that, in every city and large town in the United States, or even in any one State, there was a FREE PRESS, established by the working class, and appropriated to their interests and enlightenment: and that connected with each press there was a LIBRARY with a reading and lecturing or debating room, open every evening and on all days of relaxation from business, where working people of all descriptions might assemble, to acquire and communicate mutual information. It is more than probable, that numbers of useful labourers of all occupations would soon be induced to enter these seminaries of intelligence and virtue. The gratification necessarily arising from an enlarged and liberalized acquaintance, and from the mutual acquirement and communication of useful knowledge; the high respectability that would almost immediately attach itself to them; the certain prospect it would soon afford them of improving their future condition, and the ever increasing delight, which invariably attends a voluntarily progressive state of mental improvement, would operate as almost irresistible inducements for working people to join them.

In their public assemblies they would learn to *speak for themselves*; and with a periodical publication devoted to their instruction and mutual improvement, they would acquire the habit of *writing for themselves*. Thus they would obtain a knowledge of each other's talents, capacities and qualifications, and of course would soon begin to *nominate* candidates for public offices, *from among themselves*; men who begin their *equals* and associates, would be intimately acquainted with their wants and necessities; men who live *by their own labour*, and not upon that of others, and who *therefore* have an INTEREST perfectly in accordance with their own. These they would support through the medium of their own public journals and, being superior in numbers, with "universal suffrage," *would overcome all opposition*. The working class would then enjoy a state of political equality, and in this point of view stand upon a perfect level with the non-productive classes. They would have REAL REPRESENTATIVES, and a public opinion of their own, through which to direct and control them.

Their *true interests* also would be promoted in their legislative assemblies; for what individual, thus elected from the bosom of his associates and equals, having an interest in all points corresponding with theirs, could ever be corrupted? Or if he should, how could he return to receive the execration of the multitude, to be published as an infamous traitor and spurned with contempt by constituents, who were formerly his intimate acquaintances and friends, from those rooms where previously he used to meet them with satisfaction and gladness?

I have now endeavoured to exhibit as clear a view as I can of the different classes of men which exist in society at large; also of the character of these classes and of the relation in which they stand to each other. We have seen, nay *we do feel*, the productive and working classes toiling incessantly to produce and prepare every article of wealth for the use and enjoyment of man, which man can desire to enjoy; while themselves find it difficult to obtain a very scanty and precarious subsistence. we have seen the other classes obtaining, possessing, and enjoying, many of them in the greatest profusion, the proceeds of our labour without doing anything themselves towards producing. We have had a view of some of the principal MEANS by which this profusion of wealth is drained out of the possession of its producers, and accumulated by these classes; that is to say, by RENTS, USURY, and PROFIT.—We have seen that the present institution of *commerce*, instead of indefinitely improving the condition of mankind, is only calculated through the INCREASE OF INVENTION to plunge them into greater and greater difficulties; and that these difficulties can never be avoided, but must continue to increase without end, until either *invention* or *competition*—whichever is found to be the real cause of them—shall be driven entirely from the world. We have perceived that, through sham representation, the *real interests* and prosperity of the working class are not promoted in their legislative assemblies, and that there is no hope that they ever will be, until a UNITY OF INTERESTS shall be effected between them and their representatives. And I think we cannot but perceive, that the *chief reason* why these evils are suffered any longer to scourge us, can be found only in A GENERAL WANT OF INTELLIGENCE among the great mass of the people, relative to the *causes* of them, and to the *means* through which they may be avoided, and our true interests and real happiness secured.

AN ADDRESS

Delivered Before the Mechanics
and Working Classes Generally,
of the City and County
of Philadelphia.

At the Universalist Church,
in Callowhill Street,
on Wednesday Evening,
November 21, 1827

By the

"UNLETTERED MECHANIC"

"Then said I, Wisdom is better than Strength:
Nevertheless the poor man's wisdom is despised,
and his words are not heard."—*Ecclesiates* LX. 16

Published by Request of the
MECHANICS' DELEGATION

Printed in the Office of the Mechanics' Gazette, No. 2,
Carter's Alley.

AN ADDRESS

To the Mechanics and Working Classes

FELLOW-LABORERS

WHY on this evening do we see a numerous audience who have left the pursuits of business or recreation to assemble here? Why are the implements of handicraft laid aside or the usual resorts of pleasure neglected for the purpose of meeting in this place? Why do we see so many fellow laborers assembled on this occasion, bearing in their countenances evidence of fixed attention and deep reflection? It is because the light of reason has burst from the thralldom of ignorance, and has begun to scatter its rays on the minds of freemen! It is because the radiant beams of irresistible truth have rent the chains of error, and begun to enlighten a republican community! It is because a true knowledge of just and equal rights has commenced its march among the sons of freedom!

It is confidently hoped that the present interesting occasion will form a new epoch in the progressive march of improvement, and may it long be remembered as a time when a portion of Columbia's sons acquired fresh vigor to contend against oppression. We have met, fellow workmen, to inquire into our real condition and relative situation in society. We find ourselves oppressed on every hand—we labor hard in producing all the comforts of life for the enjoyment of others, while we ourselves obtain but a scanty portion, and even that in the present state of society depends on the will of employers. From the remote ages of antiquity, down to the present period, a large majority of the human family in all civilized nations, have been kept in a state of degradation and poverty; yet the greatness of those nations has been solely produced by that degraded and poverty-stricken majority. The boasted pyramids, monuments, temples, and statues of antiquity, owe their existence to the labors of the working class of those times. The grandeur of ancient Greece—the splendor of Rome, and the magnificence of other famed cities and nations, arose to their respective heights by the labors of hard toiling men, whose only reward was poverty, misery, and contempt! The different nations, at this period, have arrived at their present greatness and power through the labors of that class who have been unjustly divested of their richest productions, and thereby subjected to continual poverty and want. The working classes, through every age, have been the sole and only producers of the grandeur and opulence of their respective ages and nations, yet they have ever been chained down to poverty, despised and insulted by those who enjoyed a superabundance of the choicest products of their labor! The princely places, the magnificent mansions, the splendid equipages, the costly plate, the elegant and convenient furniture, with all the variety of rich and palatable viands, are solely the productions of the working class, who, after producing them, are legally but unjustly prevented from the enjoyment they yield. Whatever is enjoyed by mankind that comes under the denomination of wealth, has been produced by the labor or inventions of man; or in other words, by the working or productive class of men; yet they have ever been doomed to suffer all the evils attendant on a state of poverty and depression!

Where then has justice slept? Or in what chains has it been confined, that it has not arisen in its power, and established its immaculate laws where tyrannic oppression, and authorised extortion, have too long held mighty sway? It is the trifold band of ignorance, prejudice, and superstition, which has, for so many ages, held justice an unresisting captive.

When we look around us , my fellow workmen, we behold men on every side, enjoying wealth in all its luxuriant profusion—clothed in fine garments, and faring sumptuously every day; while we, comparatively, receive nothing but the crumbs which fall from their tables. Thousands and tens of thousands in the country are reveling in ease, and possessing in rich abundance all the comforts and luxuries which wealth is capable of affording; while we receive but the bare necessaries of life, and even many of us are driven to the depths of poverty by the present merciless system of oppression. But who produced this wealth, and all the comforts and conveniences which surround us, and of which we are deprived the privilege of partaking? Surely not those who enjoy them. There are but few indeed, who produce wealth, that ever enjoy it; while those who produce nothing, enjoy it with all its attendant blessings and comforts. In order to fully illustrate our present condition and relative situation in society, we must consider our country as containing two classes, viz.—The working or productive class, and the not-productive or accumulating class. The former class produce every article which comes under the term wealth; the latter class produce nothing valuable, but grow rich by accumulating the productions of the former, thus enjoying all the advantages and benefits of wealth which they never produced.

That labor which enriches our country, has been found by political economists, to consist of two kinds—*productive* and *official*. Productive labor is that which manufactures and prepares all the variety of articles which are used for the comfort, convenience, or pleasure of mankind. Official labor is that which is employed to convey articles of wealth from one place or country to another, for sale or exchange. By this division of the laboring class, it will be seen that productive laborers are those, and only those, who bring into existence and prepare for use, whatever is conducive to the happiness of mankind. Such are the cultivators of the soil—mechanics and tradesmen of every description—artisans, laboring men, &c. Official laborers are those employed in loading vessels, or conducting them to their destined ports; or in conveying articles of wealth to their place of destination by the different modes of inland transportation. Although official labor is a secondary employment, it is of as much importance to a city, state, or nation, as productive labor. It will appear evident to all, that productive labor must first be performed to manufacture or prepare articles of wealth, before official labor can be employed in their transportation. These two classes collectively, are admitted to constitute what is called the working class of the country. But let it be remembered, and may it be indelibly impressed on your minds, that it is those, and those alone, who actually put their hands to productive or official labor, who enrich the country and not those who employ them.* An employer who does not

---

* I am aware that many will deny this assertion, and endeavor by the aid of

regularly apply his hands to daily toil is an accumulator and not a producer of wealth: he accumulates by a profit on the labor of those in his employ, giving them a compensation barely sufficient to enable them to live, and appropriating to his own use the wealth of their productions. There are many employers who are in some degree excusable in the present state of society for thus accumulating; for instance, a large portion of master mechanics: they deal with accumulators more powerful than themselves, and therefore are not to be severely censured for the profit they make on men in their employ. Accumulation, or in other words, legal robbery,* commences with the richest class, and is continued through every grade of society till it reaches the working or productive class, but can go no further.** This latter class are deprived the means of accumulating; they have none to accumulate from; therefore they are under the absolute necessity of producing wealth, not only for themselves, but for all the different grades of accumulators above them and when each accumulator has taken his share, the real producers have but a trifle left for themselves. When a person has gathered together a large property, he is said to have made a fortune, although he may have never produced wealth to the amount of one hundred dollars during his life. Working men have made the fortune, and have been legally, but very unjustly robbed of it. But whoever acquires a fortune in the present state of society, whether he be a manu-

assertion can be proved beyond doubt or contradiction. The limits of this address will not permit me to support with undeniable evidence, all the assertions which it will be necessary to make; but may you all bear in mind, that no assertion will be made that cannot be demonstrated—nothing will be offered to you for truth, that cannot be proved beyond doubt; and proof will be adduced, should any sophistical attacks be publicly made.

* Some of our friends may complain that this language is too strong; but for my own part, I think the oppressive system we have to oppose, is so strongly fortified by custom and prejudice, that truth, in its most forcible form, is required to break down these tremendous barriers.—An experienced general would not attack a strong fortress with pop-guns fired at random; but his heaviest artillery would be brought forward, and levelled directly at the opposing obstacle. If one class of men are protected by law in taking advantage of the necessities of another class, we cannot find a more appropriate name for such conduct than legal robbery.

** Let it not be understood that we throw unlimited censure on any class of accumulators in society: The present unjust system upon which society is founded, impels them in a manner to take advantage wherever they can. But they deserve no small degree of censure, for not endeavoring to change the unjust system of individual interest and competition, which fills our country with every description of crime, and carries misery and wretchedness to every town and village.

facturer, merchant, storekeeper, or broker, or any other accumulator, he does it by legalized extortion: the laws of the country protect him in robbing the working class of their productions and appropriating them to his own use without giving an equivalent in exchange. It is doubtless well known, to every one present, that the accumulating class never put their hands to valuable labor, or if they do, it is only for experiment or amusement, and consequently too trifling to be counted as any thing towards their support; yet they live in ease, and enjoy in plenty, all the real comforts which our rich country affords, while the producers of those comforts are frequently debarred from the common necessaries of life, and still doomed to toil! But the working, or wealth producing class, support every member of the community; not only themselves, but every other class besides. The accumulating class are indebted, deeply indebted to the working class for all the wealth they enjoy. There is a class among us whose occupations impel them to perform labor, but are not to be reckoned with the working class; for instance, druggists, storekeepers, &c. must labor to keep their several commodities properly arranged, and deal them out to their customers, but their labor is not productive of a single article of wealth—every article in which they deal has been previously provided by other hands. They are paid for their labor by a profit on their articles, which pay is four, six, and often ten times the amount of that received by productive laborers.

But those who are toiling day after day, spending their strength, and wasting their health in the production of wealth, are doomed, not only to poverty with all its attendant inconveniences, but even to contempt. I appeal to you, fellow workmen, for the truth of this assertion. Can any one deny that those who enjoy in rich abundance that wealth which is produced by the hand of labor, treat us as vastly their inferiors? However fair our characters may stand for integrity, industry, and sobriety, we are not admitted into their circles, nor treated as equals on any occasion; and they even wish us to consider it a condescension when they treat us with common civility. But notwithstanding all their self assumed superiority, they are indebted to us and our fellow-laborers for all their principal enjoyments. But when unerring justice, that most exalted of all the virtues, shall establish its perfect laws in our Republic, superiority will only be confined to superior merit and usefulness.

But to bring the subject more closely to our feelings, let us confine our views to this city. Here we find merchants, wholesale and retail dealers, rich manufacturers and brokers, together with all the other different grades of accumulators and consumers, living in the enjoyment of a plentiful supply of worldly comforts and conveniences. Many of them possess these blessings in great profusion, without ever having produced a single article which they possess. They enjoy this profusion of worldly good by collecting the wealth produced by others, without making an adequate compensation for it. This accumulation is performed in various ways through the medium of rents, usury, and profit, legally wrested from hard toiling men, who are thereby reduced to poverty and treated with contempt. I do not inform, but permit me to remind you, that you have assisted your share in supplying our city with all the desirable comforts by which you are surrounded, and of which you have been deprived by authorized extortion. But why is it that we, who bring wealth into existence, are deprived of the comfort it yields? Why are we reduced to poverty, slighted and despised by those who live at ease upon the products of our labor? The answer is easy—our predecessors for want of information were blindly led to surrender up their rights to men possessing superior knowledge, and those rights can never be regained by us, until we acquire a proper knowledge of their value, and the best method to obtain them.

In order to bring this part of the subject more clearly to view, let us for a moment turn our attention to that interesting period, when the patriotic Delegates of the then Colonies assembled in yonder Hall, and boldly declared to the world, "That the United Colonies were, and of right ought to be Free and Independent States." That same august and venerated Delegation asserted the self evident truths, "that *all men were created equal*; that they are endowed with certain *unalienable rights*; that among these are life, liberty, and the pursuit of happiness."[1] They mutually pledged their "lives, their fortunes, and their sacred honor" to secure those rights, and their coadjutors in the cause of liberty gave their blood and their lives to maintain them. But those equal rights which were at that time asserted, and purchased with blood and treasure, are not enjoyed at the present period by a majority of

American citizens. Every candid and reflecting mind must admit, that the working class of our country do not enjoy the rights of liberty and equality.

If the wealth producing class had claimed their rights at the birth of our national liberty, and maintained them unimpaired to this day, we should not have been in our present degraded condition. But for the want of information relative to their rights and powers, they were controlled by those possessing superior skill, who assumed the power of forming laws which have ever since chained the working class down to poverty. For the want of knowledge among our predecessors, they were led to surrender their rights to the non-productive and accumulating class, and thereby subjected themselves to degradation and oppression, which has been handed down to us, and will continue to grow deeper and more severe until we shall obtain the requisite information to claim and possess those rights. Thus we find that the true source of our present depression was a lack of necessary information among the former working classes of our country. As the evils we now suffer originated in the want of knowledge, they will of course continue to increase upon us until we arm ourselves with sufficient information to destroy them. The wisest men have declared that knowledge is power; and when we shall have obtained a true knowledge of our importance in society, and our just rights, we shall then make use of our power to possess them. Then, and not till then, shall we enjoy the full value of our productions, and hold that elevated rank in society to which we are justly entitled.

The limits of this address will not permit me to commence an illustrative enquiry into the variety of circumstances which have brought us to our present depressed situation; neither is it my intention to fully explain the variety of ways by which we are divested of our productions; nor point out all the evils that exist in society in relation to us. We know that we suffer numerous evils; we know that we are unjustly divested of the productions of our labor by the sanction of custom and legal authority; and we know we are slighted and despised, (however fair our moral characters may stand) by those who live in ease upon the wealth we produce, thus adding insult to injury. Then let us rather endeavor to seek a remedy for these evils, than search to ascertain how they came. The original cause of our degradation has already been pointed out, and also some of the evils which we actually suffer, but to give a particular description of each, and their causes, all of which have grown out of the original cause, would require a volume. A few more will be shown as the nature of the subject may require. It is presumed that many fellow-workmen in this assembly are not aware that the compensation which they actually enjoy, is trifling indeed compared with the wealth they produce. Take the working class of this City and County collectively, and where they produce wealth to the value of ten dollars, they do not actually enjoy more than the amount of one dollar.[2] Perhaps this assertion will appear extravagant to many in this audience, and probably its authenticity will be questioned by some avaricious accumulator. Should any such doubt about this assertion, let him be informed that your speaker holds himself in readiness to prove it by incontrovertible evidence.

It has been previously stated to you this evening, that every article of wealth of whatever description, whether of luxury, comfort, or convenience, has been produced solely by the working class. Is there an accumulator who can deny this? If any one attempt to deny it, let him first ask himself who produced the various articles which he enjoys, and let his conscience answer the important question. If then every article of wealth which is enjoyed in our City is furnished by the working class, and they who produced this wealth received by a humble subsistence, must it not appear evident, that when taken *collectively*, they produce wealth to the value of more then ten dollars for every dollar which themselves enjoy? It will readily be admitted that some trades of the working class receive more in proportion to their productions than what has been stated; others again receive less. But the evils which we suffer are too numerous to be particularized, and clearly exposed on this occasion; but I trust it will be done on some future occasion like the present, or through the medium of a newspaper about to be established by the sanction of Mechanics. In the mean time I would recommend you, my fellow-workmen, to investigate the subject yourselves, and converse upon it with your friends, and search out the various channels by which you are drained of the wealth you produce. Let it be the theme of your meditations when alone, and the topic of conversation when in company. Let the usual subjects of amusement, pleasure, and recreation be laid aside for the more important one of your rights and interests. By pursuing such a course, you will learn your real value and importance in society, and become acquainted with your just and equal rights as freeborn citizens. By thus investigating the subject, you will learn the various ways by which you are legally but unjustly divested of the products of your labor, and chained to continual toil, and hopeless poverty. By such a course, you will become more and more acquainted with the best means of raising yourselves from degradation and poverty, to high respectability and plenty. Then let this subject be first in our private thoughts, and first in our open conversations. Our degradation, oppression, and poverty, will be continually increasing with the increase of the working population; and it is well known that their augmentation by natural increase and by emigration from Europe, is much more rapid than the other class. It will then appear evident to all who will give the subject a few moments' consideration, that in the present conflicting system of society, the rapid increase of the working class, together with the introduction of labor-saving machines, will lessen the demand for manual labor, and consequently diminish it in price. The other class, who collect and consume wealth without ever producing it, are ever ready to take advantage of us whenever it is in their power, and we find they do not fail to avail themselves of these circumstances, and reduce the price of labor as low as possible. But it is frequently said by those who live upon the working class without working themselves, that every sober, honest, industrious man can at all times procure a comfortable living for himself and his family, by his labor. Such an assertion is either a wilful misrepresentation or is made through ignorance. There are hundreds of sober industrious men, who seek employment for weeks before they obtain it. How can such men obtain a comfortable living at all times, unless they obtain it on credit? It is true that some are so fortunate as to obtain constant employ, but their pay for the most part, is no more that sufficient for their subsistence; and if they are attacked by a lengthy illness, they must depend on the cold charity of the world for all the comforts they obtain, and this too, after having produced wealth to six times the value of what they ever received!

It is an unfortunate circumstance, that too many of our fellow workmen have imagined their increasing oppression to be an evil for which no remedy could be found;—too many have quietly settled down into submission under this fatal idea, and believing their difficulties must continue to increase without remedy, have resorted to the intoxicating bowl to drown the sense of approaching distress. But permit me to inform, nay, boldly to declare without fear of contradictory evidence, that there is not a moral evil in society for which no remedy can be found; the grand difficulty, is, people will not resort to the remedy. The idea that we must of necessity submit to tyrannic oppression, legalized robbery, and severe privations, because our numbers are increasing more rapidly than the other class, is next to the height of folly. The doctrine of necessary evil, which many appear to believe, and some have advocated, is as destitute of foundation as the mind which first conceived it. I bid a proud defiance to the united talents of this country, to point out a moral evil in society which is necessary, or one for which no remedy can be found. If we still continue to suffer the evils which are yearly increasing upon us in number and magnitude, we must suffer them because we will not apply the proper remedy, and not because there is no remedy for us.

Several of the different trades of our city have at various former periods attempted to meliorate their depressed condition by forming themselves into societies, and adopting such measures as were thought most conducive to their interests and prosperity. They have sometimes succeeded in obtaining a trifling advance of wages, but that trifling advantage has generally been of short duration, being soon wrested from them by avaricious accumulators and ungenerous employers; and never as yet , have they obtained any thing permanent. The failure of almost all former efforts to remedy our condition, has discouraged many from attempting any thing further, but let us bear in mind that the truly courageous are never discouraged by defeat. We have never as yet resorted to the proper remedy: we have only been lopping off the branches of the evil, which immediately shoot forth again— let us henceforth aim our blows at the root, and thus at once destroy both root and branch.

The formation of societies, and standing out for wages, hours, although it may serve a trifling temporary good purpose, is at best but poor patch work to cobble up a condition so tattered as ours. Some more powerful and efficient remedy must be applied, before we can reasonably hope for better times. Before proceeding to point out the only effectual and efficient measures to improve our condition, I must crave your indulgence while I make a short digression.

There are three classes of men among us, who are in duty bound to use their every exertion, and devote their best talents to restore to us our rights and privileges; but this duty they have not performed, nor have we much reason to believe they ever will. These three classes are the legislative, judicial, and theological. These classes, like many others, are solely supported by the working class. In whatever way, or from whatever hands they obtain their emoluments and salaries, their pay is produced by, and taken out of, the productions of the working class. None of them can deny this with the smallest appearance of truth. How great then are their obligations towards us; and how little, how trifling the benefit that we receive from them. The legislative class are bound by every imposing obligation of duty, to frame such laws as will secure to every man *equal rights and privileges among his fellow men*—such laws as will not permit one man to take the productions of another, without returning him an equivalent for them. But instead of doing this, they have framed laws which in their nature bind the sole producers of wealth down to poverty. They have framed laws which protect all the non-productive classes in divesting us of the productions of our labor without returning us an equal quantity of wealth in exchange. They have framed laws which authorize idle accumulators and consumers to rob us of all the most desirable comforts and conveniences of life which our own hands have produced by giving us in exchange a bare humble subsistence. They have either framed or assented to such laws which were previously framed, contrary to every principle of duty and justice.* But let us not too severely censure those who act from long established custom.

---

* Perhaps some of our friends will think it little short of high treason to speak against the laws of our country, which they say are as free as the air we breathe; but let them not condemn us too hastily. The laws of this country protect the rich in taking advantage of the necessities of the poor—they protect accumulators in robbing the real producers, and protect any person who has money, in robbing the unfortunate poor, the widow and the orphan. Are such laws just? Show me the justice of such laws, and I will recant.

Perhaps some of them will say that we have not the least reason to complain of injustice—that we agree to work for such prices as are offered, and are paid all we agree to work for. Or they may say that when we rent a house, or purchase such articles as we need, that we agree to give the sum that is charged, and therefore have no reason to complain of what we have agreed to perform. If such reasoning as this is brought against us, let us examine its consistency.—When the daring robber presents the loaded pistol to a traveller, and demands his money, threatening instant death in case of refusal, the traveller agrees to give up his property; but does that prove the robber innocent because the traveller agreed to his demands? Or does it prove that the traveller has no just reason of complaint? The traveller consents to give up his money to save his life, and our situation is very similar to his. Necessity compels us to work for such prices as are offered, and pay such prices as are demanded for every thing we need; we must either do thus—resort to fraud or theft, or perish by hunger and nakedness. Where then is the difference between our relative situation and the accumulating class, and the traveller with the highwayman? There is this difference: Our robbers are legally authorized to rob us, but the highwayman has not yet been legally authorized to rob in the manner he does,—he might be with as much justice. But all the *leading* members of legislative bodies belong to the accumulating class. They are not producers of wealth—they don't put their hands to labor; therefore they conceive their interests to be at variance with ours, and will of course support such laws as favor themselves and their class at our expense. They are nominated by accumulators, and controlled by their opinions; therefore we have no reason to suppose they will enact laws favorable to our interests although the majority who elect and support them are working men.

Next are the Judicial class—those appointed to act in the distribution of public justice. It is needless to say any thing further of this class at present, than that the working class seldom receive any other justice from them, than just punishment when they deserve it. The third class who are in duty bound to use their influence to remedy our degraded condition, is the Theological; those who are styled the servants and ambassadors of the Most High, and disciples of him whose high command declares, *"Thou shalt love thy neighbor as thyself."* They profess to be the imitators of those primitive christians who had "all things common;" among whom no idle accumulator was allowed to rob the hard toiling producer by way of profits, rents, and usury. By the nature of their profession and high calling, they are bound by the most sacred obligations, not only to teach evangelical truths, but to teach the absolute necessity of undeviating justice between man and man in all their dealings with each other. It is true that they frequently exhort mankind to deal justly, but this is not a sufficient discharge of their duty. Why do they not point out the enormous injustice of one class of men possessing legal authority to take advantage of these necessities of another? Why do they not exhibit in all its deformity, the unjust system of one class of men having power to accumulate the products of another class? Why do they not direct the power of their reasoning, and the thunders of their eloquence against the unjust and vice-creating system of conflicting interest—a system so directly opposed to that adopted by the immediate followers of the Prince of Peace?

Not all the fervent intercessions of prayer, nor all the influence of pathetic exhortation, nor all the declarations of divine denunciation, can ever arrest the progress of sin while the system of individual interest and competition is supported. If any theologians doubt this assertion, let them candidly and honestly investigate the subject before they deny its authenticity, and they will find that almost every moral evil in society has its origin in this destructive system.

Abolish this system, and crimes and misery will scarcely be known; but while it is permitted to hold its destructive reign, all efforts to stay the progress of transgression will be little better than useless. The blasting influence of conflicting interests and competition is seen and felt, in every grade of society. It strips man of all the noblest faculties of his mind, and the most exalted virtues of his heart, and leaves him an easy prey to hypocrisy, dishonesty, fraudulence, and injustice. It is the fell destroyer of all moral excellence. It is the mainspring of intemperance, theft, robbery, and murder; its malign infection has extended through the whole human family, nor does it end here—even the brightness of religion, that celestial essence, has not escaped its blasting power. These, my friends are bold assertions, and are made, not without fear of contradiction, but without fear of contradictory evidence.

If then the clergy would arrest the fatal march of vice, let them direct their attacks to its fountain head. Let them exert their talents and influence to destroy a system so fraught with almost irresistible temptations to vice. The grand nursery of sin must be destroyed before they can cherish any reasonable hopes of a general and permanent reformation in our country. If they wish to see the day of manifest glory approaching, let them devote their labors to the destruction of a system so opposed to that happy period. Let us hope that ere long shall see their talents, their learning, and their influence, directed against the mainspring of all evil, and source of every crime. Let us hope that the importance of the subject will invite them to a candid investigation, and if they sincerely wish to see religion extend, and flourish in all its sublime and harmonious beauties, we may reasonably hope that ere long they will be found the strenuous advocates of mutual, instead of conflicting interest.

I trust you will all pardon this digression which appeared so necessary to our subject. There is no class in society who feel the severity of the conflicting and competing system so much ourselves: almost the whole of its enormous and deadly weight falls upon us, crushing us down to hopeless poverty; and if we have no advocates in the Legislative, Judicial, nor Theological class, it is time to examine what powers we yet possess of our own to destroy this fatal evil.

We yet possess the right of suffrage—the right of electing our own legislators and rulers. This right has not as yet been wrested from our hands, but unless we soon make a better use of it than we ever have done, we have great reason to fear that it will be lost to us forever. The right of giving our votes to whom we please, and a knowledge to use this right in a proper manner, are the only effectual remedies for improving our depressed condition. Then let us apply these remedies to our own advantage, before we are deprived of such a privilege by aristocratical accumulators. We have too long been deluded by those who live in ease and grow rich by our productions, and have suffered ourselves to be blindly led to support men for office whose interest in the present state of society, is directly opposed to our own. All our legislators and rulers are nominated by the accumulating class, and controlled by their opinions—how then can we expect that laws will be framed which will favor our interest? The men who nominate, and those who are chosen, do not live by productive labor; therefore their interest is in direct opposition to ours, and of course they will frame and support such laws as will give them unjust superiority over us. Designing and interested politicians will blazen virtues which their favorite candidates never possessed, and proclaim in impressive language, patriotism which modern candidates have never felt. The little good which a candidate may have done, will be swelled to a mountain by those of his adherents who hope to reap a benefit by his election, while all his crimes, either of a moral or political nature, will be diminished to a mole-hill, or enveloped in the mantle of sophistry. We have too long been deceived by designing men of both political parties; they have told us what fine things their favorite candidates would do if elected, and what excellent times it would be for working people throughout the country. But I candidly ask you, my fellow-laborers, have we ever seen their political predictions fulfilled? We never have. The men whom we have been told would do so much for the working class, have frequently been elected by both political parties, but what have they ever done? Our general situation is growing worse and worse every year. How long, my fellow-workmen, shall we suffer ourselves to be deceived? How long shall we be blindly led to support men for office whose interest is opposed to ours? How long shall we suffer brainless zeal to take command of our sober senses, and lead us headlong to espouse the cause of men, who consider us unworthy of any further notice than to gain our good will for the purpose of obtaining our votes? Is it not high time that we begin to reflect on these things? Let us now begin to learn wisdom by dear bought experience, and no longer support men who adopt no measures to support us. We have not the least reason to expect that men who do not live by the labor of their own hands, will ever study the interests of those who do. They live upon the productions of the working class, without producing any thing valuable themselves; and if they did not keep us chained down to toil and poverty, they would soon be obliged to apply their own hands to labor in order to live. It is very evident, my friends, that those who do not live by producing wealth themselves, certainly live by accumulating the productions of the working or wealth producing class; and consequently they conceive it their interest to keep us in a state of humble dependence.

And it makes not the least difference to us, which political party obtains the sway in government so long as they are accumulators, and are nominated and controlled by accumulators. Nor does it make any difference whether rich master mechanics and manufacturers, or lawyers and merchants are elected to office; they are all accumulators. and of course will feel it their interest to keep the actual producers in ignorance and poverty. If we send men to the legislature who encourage American manufacturers of every kind, it is only advantageous to those who have a capital sufficient to establish themselves in business to a considerable extent, and add to their capital by a profit on those in their employ; but the actual working class are not in the least benefitted by such measures; they must still work on for such prices as their employers are pleased to give, which is never more than sufficient for a subsistence.

Then let us no longer be deluded by false arguments and false zeal to vote for this man or that man, or this or that party, for our interest is never taken into consideration by any one of them—they only talk about it to keep us in delusion. Let us then "be wise in time." We belong to the majority of the community, and possess the constitutional right of electing our own rulers; then let us unite in the exercise of this right to our advantage, and no longer let the opposing class allure us to support their interests at the expense of our own. By electing representatives who are vowed friends to our interest, they will of course legislate in our favor, and we shall then have laws which will give us equal privileges with the other class in all respects, and place us on an equality with them in every point of view. We shall then have laws which will not protect them in divesting us of the productions of our labor, without returning us an equal value.* Then let us resolve to never more give our suffrages to any but members of the working class, or to such others as will publicly pledge themselves to support our interest in the legislative Hall. But perhaps our opposing class will tell us that we have no men capable of legislating, and directing the civil affairs of the coun-

---

* It is very plausible, fellow workmen, that we shall be denounced as a band of "*levellers;*" but let it be understood that we have no wish to bring any one down to the level with ourselves, for we are much lower in the scale of society, than we wish any of our fellow creature to be. Our object is to bring ourselves up to a level with any other class, but if any one can show us we are in error, we will immediately desist.

try; that it requires men of learning, who have long been conversant with state affairs, and studied the laws of other nations. They may tell us that working men have never had opportunities to qualify themselves for legislators, however bright their natural talents may be. I frankly admit that it requires men well learned in all the arts of false reasoning and skilled in all the deceptive political maneovres of monarchies to legislate, and keep in countenance laws to support the present system of robbery and oppression. But permit me to remind you that it requires no extraordinary qualification to enact laws which shall give every member of the human family equal rights and privileges among his fellow men in every respect, and protect the weak against the machinations of the strong. No extraordinary effort of the mind is required to pursue the plain simple path of truth and justice; but mankind seem to possess such a propensity for mysteries, that in framing laws, as well as in other things, they have left the plain artless rules of consistency, and wandered into mystical absurdities. Thus many of our laws are mysterious and inconsistent, and it requires men of more artful ingenuity than the working class, to keep such laws in countenance. The working class, it is true, have never had opportunities to qualify themselves for managing inconsistencies with dexterity, nor are they skilled in making injustice and extortion appear like just and equal rights; but I trust many of them are fully competent to legislate upon the plain rules of justice and equity. But admitting that there is none among us who are sufficiently qualified for legislation, we have every reason to believe that we are not destitute of firm friends in the other class, who, if elected by us, would be the unshaken advocates of our rights in the Hall of legislation. But it is hoped that no working man will suffer himself to be led by persuasion, or drove by threats, to vote for any candidate of either party, unless such candidates stand publicly pledged to advocate our equal rights.

Should we unite in the plan which I have suggested, no obstacle can oppose our elevation to an equal rank with any class in society; but we must expect that those who feel an interest in keeping us chained to slavery and ignorance, will use all the means in their power to divert us from the object. We must expect to be assailed on every side by false reasonings and artful persuasions, by erroneous conclusions drawn from sophistical arguments, and by prediction of some direful event which will attend us if we persevere. But let us pay no regard to those who would attempt to draw us aside from our duty—a duty we owe to ourselves and our posterity. Our cause is a good one; it is the cause of humanity, of justice and of truth. Then let us pursue, with unshaken perseverance, the grand object of obtaining our just rights and rank in society by lawful means. Let us arm ourselves with the power of knowledge, and obtain a bloodless victory over legal oppression, and authorized extortion. There is no other way to effectually and permanently improve our condition, but to elect for our civil rulers, men who are avowed friends to our rights, and stand publicly pledged to support them. We must elect men who are friends to equal rights in the true sense of these words; and who will not give the rich employer authority to take advantage of the necessities of the employed. The formation of Trade societies, and standing out for high wages, or a more limited number of working hours, will never accomplish any permanent good. I would not be understood to discourage such societies; they will no doubt serve a temporary good purpose, and afford us means of obtaining a part of our just dues as productive members of the community. The formation of societies by every different occupation of the working class, I would strongly recommend,—that being the ground work, the solid foundation of the plan we must pursue to arrive at our object. Several of the different trades of this city and county have already formed societies, and appointed Delegates who meet in convention, and devise plans and means for the welfare of their respective societies. There are some societies which are not as yet represented in this delegation, and several trades not yet formed into societies, but it is hoped they will all see and feel the importance of such measures, and specially take the proper steps to send their Delegates. I would most earnestly recommend all the various occupations of the working classes, to form themselves into societies without delay, and adopt a suitable constitution and by-laws to secure mutual harmony and good order in each society, and between each society; and let every society send its quota of Delegates to the General Convention. "When the different branches or occupations of the working class have formed societies, and properly organized themselves, the first difficulty in our way will be overcome. I would then recommend that one

Delegate from each society be appointed to form a committee, whose duty it shall be to select and nominate candidates for the National or State Legislatures, and other civil officers. When suitable candidates have been selected, let them be recommended to each trade society, and let every working man come forward to their support, and success will inevitably crown the effort.

The foregoing plan is not recommended as the most suitable one that could be devised; it is only recommended for your consideration, with the hope that much improvement will be made upon it. The formation of societies by every occupation of working men is deemed indispensably necessary; when that has been done, other suitable measures will no doubt present themselves and can be adopted.

As one of the best means of meliorating our condition is the acquisition of useful knowledge, I must essentially recommend you to the advantages now presented by the Mechanics' Library Company of this City for acquiring such knowledge.[3] While we are destitute of useful knowledge, we can never arrive to any degree of eminence in society. A general diffusion of information among us is of the first importance, for without it we shall never be able to conceive and digest the most suitable plans for our improvement. If by some mighty effort, or some fortunate circumstance, we should obtain our just and equal rights, we should never be able to retain them without a competent knowledge of their value, and the best means of securing them. We should be liable at any time have them wrested from our hands by those possessing superior skill, and again be subjected to depression, toil, and poverty. Then let it be forcibly impressed on our minds, that a more general diffusion of knowledge among us is absolutely necessary. The Library Company now possess the means of diffusing much useful information to every working man who will avail himself of its advantages. It now contains a choice collection of books, with valuable and useful periodical journals, calculated to afford both knowledge and amusement. It is open every day and evening, and every member when he finds leisure, can enjoy its advantages. Debates are held at the Library Rooms every Wednesday evening; the subjects of discussion generally turn on the best methods to improve the condition of the working classes. These debates are both instructive and edifying, and calculated to lead the mind to useful enquiries.

Permit me then, my fellow-laborers to urge you to avail your-selves of the advantages now offered by the Institution just men-tioned. The initiation fee is but one dollar, and the benefits to be obtained are greater than can be computed at present. Shall it be said that an institution presenting so many important advantages to working men is neglected? Shall we refuse to accept the valu-able privileges now offered to us for a trifle? Shall we refuse to avail ourselves of the means of acquiring that knowledge which is so important to our best interests and prosperity? While we neglect to store our minds with useful information, we can never rise above our present condition, for ignorance will inevitably render all our efforts useless. Therefore, let us diligently and per-severingly apply ourselves to the acquisition of more useful knowledge than we yet have done, and we can then bid defiance to oppression and poverty.

The wisest men of every age have considered knowledge as power; it gives mankind a power vastly superior to bodily strength, and enables them to make even the laws of nature sub-servient to their happiness. But the acquirement of knowledge is vain, unless it is directed to the general good of society. If we should attain the wisdom of the most wise, and prostrate that wisdom before the shrine of intemperance or avarice, it would be entirely useless. We shall never gain any profitable knowledge by applying to the "social glass" or gaming table, or any other pursuits of the like nature.... Let us seek that superior happiness which is to be found in storing the mind with useful knowledge, and in social intercourse with the virtuous and moral part of society. In such a course of life we shall find enjoyments vastly superior to any that can be enjoyed over what is falsely called the friendly glass, or any other pursuits of that nature. If we wish to rise above our present state, and enjoy an equality with the other classes, we must render ourselves worthy of such an elevation, or we shall never be able to obtain it. We must also divest ourselves of every thing mean and vulgar, and no longer speak contemptu-ously of our fellow-workmen, because they do not follow the same occupation as ourselves. We must no longer cherish the vulgar idea, that one occupation is more respectable than an-other. The idea that some occupations are more respectable than others, originated in pride and ignorance. No one occupation can make a man any more respectable than another; he must make himself so, or he cannot deserve respect. If we allow truth and justice to speak, they will tell us that even the occupation of a laborer is as respectable as any other, although it is falsely considered otherwise. The laboring man who renders himself a worthy and useful member in society, as far as his circumstances will permit, is deserving far more respect than the most ingenious artisan who is addicted to the "social glass" and gaming table. We must respect every fellow-workman, of whatever occupation, according to his merits and usefulness, or we never can become united as a body; and unless we are united in our efforts, we shall never succeed in rising above our present condition. We must cast away all vulgar prejudices which had their origin in false pride and ignorance, and hail every well disposed fellow-workman as a brother. The different trades can never become united, so long as the members of one trade consider themselves better than those of another; and without a union of the different trades, we must ever remain the slaves of accumulators. When we can become united like a band of brothers in claiming our equal rights, oppression will begin to totter on its throne, and extortion tremble on its rotten seat. Monopoly will hide its hideous form from the glance of contempt, while equality, justice, harmony, and happiness will unfurl their peaceful banners over the community.

We have now, my fellow-laborers, taken a general view of our true condition and relative situation in society. We have seen that all wealth is the production of the working class of the country, and that we have assisted our share in producing the wealth by which we are surrounded. We have also seen that we are legally, but unjustly, robbed of the greatest part of the wealth we produce through the medium of profits, rents, and interest: and we have likewise seen, that the present existing laws, formed and supported by accumulators, authorise them to take advantage of our necessities, and keep us chained to poverty. We find that the evils which oppress us must continue to increase unless we, apply the proper remedy to remove them. I have endeavored to lay before you a general outline of the most effectual and permanent remedies for improving our condition, and placing us on an equality with the accumulating class in every point of view. It now remains for us to decide whether we will apply these remedies or not.

In my attempts to point out the best means of meliorating our condition, I have not gone into particulars—the limits of this address would not permit it. If we can unite in electing such men to office as are openly avowed friends to our rights and interest, our greatest difficulty will be overcome; we can then take such other steps as circumstances may require, and rise to the possession of plenty and happiness, in spite of opposing obstacles. I have only to add, that by a union of efforts we shall inevitably rise to an equality of rights with all its attendant blessings; but without our united efforts, we shall continue to fall still lower in the scale of society, and sink still deeper in poverty.

*   *   *

P.S. The author holds himself pledged to the public (if life and health are spared him) to show that the system of equality advocated in the foregoing address can easily be made practicable without injuring any individual in society. This will be done through the medium of the *Mechanics' Gazette*.[4]*

* Pamphlet, Copy in Library of Company of Philadelphia.

Working People's Movements

The leaders of the two great political parties appear to feel a deep interest in the present efforts of the Working People, to form themselves into a distinct party. The friends of the Administration, anxious to gain as much as possible from their movements, have tried every means to divert them from their real object, and draw them within the sphere of their own influence; whilst the leaders of the opposing party have manifested equal agitation lest the Working People become successful. In one thing, however, we believe they both agree, to wit, in their dread of our forming a party, *distinct from, and independent of, themselves.* If it is not so, why attempt, on one side, to cajole us from the pursuit of our own proper political interests, and render us mere tools for supporting their measures. And why, on the other side, deprecate, insult, and brow-beat us for pursuing measures which we believe absolutely necessary to insure an honest exercise of legislative power, with a real equality of rights, and the means of enjoyment to the American people? These efforts, however, on either side, are not likely to succeed. So far from the Working People feeling themselves "degraded" by being separated from their idle, intriguing and ambitious oppressors, of both parties, who have hitherto swayed them as mere tools for the promotion of their private interest and aggrandizement, they are every where beginning to rejoice in the opportunity now afforded them to effect their long wished for emancipation.

As conductors of a journal exclusively devoted to the enlightenment and prosperity of the working classes, we feel it our duty to vindicate them from the foul charges and assertions that have been made by aristocrats and politicians (not working men) who are neither acquainted with the nature of their true interests, nor appear desirous of promoting them. We wish it understood, however, that our present contest is with *principle*, not *persons*; as it is our intention that nothing of a personal character shall ever disgrace our columns.

1st. We are told, that "our Constitution and *Laws* are made to prevent any *distinctions* among the people." If by the word "distinctions" is meant mere names or *titles*, the position may stand good; but if we are to understand distinctions in *reality*, in *fact*, and not the mere shadow, then it is without foundation; for every man of common sense knows that there exists *as real* a distinction between the sons of poverty and toil, who earn their bread by the sweat of their brow; whose limited information and knowledge, (if they are not left the victims of total ignorance) must be derived through the degrading medium of legislative charities, in the form of public schools; and the haughty favorites of wealth and science, who riot in idleness and luxury, accumulating their country's wealth through the medium of *law-supported monopolies* and speculation, as exists in any other country. Have not our legislators, by LAWS DIRECT, created almost innumerable banking and monopolizing institutions; and clothed them with *distinct* and exclusive powers and privileges—institutions that are rapidly accumulating nearly all the *land, capital, national or public improvements*, and *labour* of the country to themselves? And while these privileged aristocracies, *created by law*, are monopolizing the wealth and power of the nation, is it not a fact that the mass of the people—the *working people*, are every year growing poorer, and more subject to the influence of these privileged classes, and to that of rich individual capitalists, who can at all times take them like mere vassals, into their employment, or turn them out of it at *pleasure*? These, institutions (the members of which require nothing to constitute them dukes, lords, &c. but the mere titles) are already formed into powerful aristocracies in every portion of our country and, unless their powers are checked by legislators chosen by the people, they bid fair, at no distant period, to combine their forces to crush our republican institutions, and utterly destroy the freedom we now possess in the choice of our legislators—bid fair, in fact, to constitute themselves our tyrants both in name and reality, and lay all our boasted liberties in the dust. And yet we are told, openly told, the barefaced falsehood, that "our laws are all made to *prevent* distinctions among the people, and that the poor and rich are *equal* objects of their care!" Can the authors of such statements be men of republican principles?

2nd—It is asserted that "the working classes have assumed an attitude *hostile* to the constitution and to our republican institutions." This, if we mistake not, we can prove to be a libel and vile slander on the recent efforts of the working people of this city and country. The attitude assumed by these consists simply in holding public meetings to effect a nomination of candidates to represent them in the various public offices of the state. Does the constitution forbid their holding such meetings? Does it declare that the majority of the people shall not exercise the right of nominating their public officers? No, it is the tyrant only who would rob them of that right. When have the working people said to the *lawyer* or the merchant, you shall not nominate your public officers? No, we wish not to limit the rights or the privileges of any class of citizens—we say to all, nominate whom you please; but do not restrain or limit us. We say to the rich accumulator, your interest is opposed to ours, and legislators of your selection will be such and will promote *your interests* at the expense of ours, therefore, whom you nominate, *we will not nominate*; whom you vote for, *we will not vote for*; and where is the man who will tell us, You shall do it? That man is a tyrant, and gives evidence that he would rob us of our rights both of nominating and voting, if he could do it. The constitution guarantees to every citizen the free and unrestrained choice, both of nominating and voting for whomsoever he wishes to represent him; and whoever he is that abuses the working classes for delegating their power of nomination, to men of their own appointment, is their enemy.

3d—It is said, "that the rights of ALL are sacredly guaranteed and assiduously promoted by our laws." And again, "what man is there that can say as a working man—I am without protection." He can make such an assertion, and ask such a question, proves himself destitute of every spark of information relative to the interests, the rights, and the welfare of the working classes. Go! son of aristocracy! survey the desolate and heart-sickening abodes of hundreds of *weavers*, who inhabit the precincts of this city! who, by the most life consuming exertions, are unable to earn more than three or four dollars per week!—Whole families, who are sunk below all human enjoyment and all human hope—

too poor to subscribe for the means of information, and left by iron hearted legislation, in a state of too much ignorance to appreciate its inestimable value; then turn your eyes on a few rich capitalists, who through the medium of *monopolies*, have appropriated to themselves, and are accumulating all the means by which this useful class of citizens were formerly rendered comfortable, and blush for the ignorance manifested in such assertions and such questions. We mention the weavers because we have witnessed with feelings indescribable, the horrible oppression which grinds them into the dust of poverty. But they are not the only class. The hatters of this city are at this moment suffering under similar evils from a similar cause, only in a less intolerable degree. The surplus producers of these and other trades, are already crowding into other occupations, and the working classes are beginning every where to groan under the increasing evil. And while it continues to be the order of legislation, in accordance with the wishes of the great, to encourage monopoly and oppress the people, we ask, where is the evil likely to terminate? Not till it arrives at a state of tyranny and oppression, of wealth to the few and misery to the multitude, beyond any thing which has ever yet been exhibited in the annals of time. "The rights of *all* promoted, and the working man protected!" We cannot suppress our indignation at a libel so insulting to the feelings, the common sense, and the bitter experience of the working classes.

We are sorry to trespass so long on the patience of our readers—we must, therefore, just glance at the other charges which come under our notice, as briefly as possible.

It is not true, then that "the leaders of the administration are also the leaders of these deluded Operatives"—or that "we cannot be more fairly or more justly represented than we now *are!*" It is not true, that a line of distinction drawn between the industrious producers of the nation's wealth and the idle accumulators of it, "degrades" the former, and "concedes the point of superiority in the idle classes." It is an aristocratic and insulting sentiment, which declares that honest industry derives any degree of respectability whatever, from a connexion with imperious oppressors and useless idlers;—or that it becomes in the smallest degree "degraded" by annihilating such a pernicious connexion. For, reasoning by inference, if the industrious authors of their country's wealth, could be elevated in character by an intimate politi-cal connexion with the proud, the idle, and the aristocratic, but *untitled* plunderers (by law) of the wealth; how much more must they be exalted by adding to their legal plunderers the titles of lord, duke, king, father in God, noble, excellency, esquire, &c. And if the working classes can be gulled into a belief of the first position, how long is it likely to be before we may expect the latter one to be forced upon them? Every Operative common sense, can see that such sentiments are as opposed to truth and to real Republicanism, as darkness is to light.

And lastly, it is not true that the authors of such sentiments, be they who they may, can be the sincere friends of the working classes as such; nor is it possible that they ever should be, while they possess such a limited knowledge of what constitutes their rights, just claims, and interests.

In conclusion, we cannot but express a hope that the Working Classes will not suffer themselves to be brow beat from the noble stand they have, manfully taken; but, inasmuch as the working man's tickets, will extend no further than to *state affairs*, and will have no connexion whatever with the presidential question, we hope they will come forward on the day of election, and from their independence by *voting their own ticket.*

Mechanics' Free Press, September 20, 1828

REPORT OF THE WORKING MEN'S COMMITTEE ON PUBLIC EDUCATION[1]

February, 1830

Report of the Joint Committees of the City and County of Philadelphia, appointed September, 1829, to ascertain the state of public instruction in Pennsylvania, and to digest and propose such improvements in education as may be deemed essential to the intellectual and moral prosperity of the people.

It is now nearly five months since the committees were appointed to cooperate on this arduous duty. But the importance of the subject, the time expended in research and enquiry, in order to procure information relative to it; and the multiplied discussions and deliberations necessary to reconcile and correct their own different and sometimes conflicting views, will, they believe, constitute a reasonable apology for this long delay.

After devoting all the attention to the subject, and making every enquiry which their little leisure and ability would permit, they are forced into the conviction, that there is great defect in the educational system of Pennsylvania; and that much remains to be accomplished before it will have reached that point of improvement which the resources of the state would justify, and which the intellectual condition of the people and the preservation of our republican institutions demand.

With the exception of this city and county, the city and incorporated borough of Lancaster, and the city of Pittsburgh, erected into "school districts" since 1818, it appears that the entire state is destitute of any provisions for public instruction, except those furnished by the enactment of 1809.[2] This law requires the assessors of the several counties to ascertain and return the number of children whose parents are unable, through poverty, to educate them; and such children are permitted to be instructed at the most convenient schools at the expense of their respective counties.

The provisions of this act, however, are incomplete and frequently inoperative. They are, in some instances, but partially executed; in others, perverted and abused—and in many cases entirely and culpably neglected. The funds appropriated by the act, have, in some instances, been embezzled by fraudulent agents; and in others, partial returns of the children have been made, and some have been illegally and intentionally excluded from participating in the provisions of the law. From a parsimonious desire of saving the county funds, the cheapest, and consequently the most inefficient schools have been usually selected by the commissioners of the several counties.

The elementary schools throughout the state are irresponsible institutions, established by individuals, from mere motives of private speculation or gain, who are sometimes destitute of character, and frequently, of the requisite attainments and abilities. From the circumstance of the schools being the absolute property of individuals, no supervision or effectual control can be exercised over them; hence, ignorance, inattention, and even immorality, prevail to a lamentable extent among their teachers.

In some districts, no schools whatever exist! No means whatever of acquiring education are resorted to; while ignorance, and its never failing consequence, crime, are found to prevail in these neglected spots, to a greater extent than in other more favored portions of the state.

The "three school districts," however, which have been alluded to, are not liable to these objections. Much good, in particular, has resulted from the establishment of the first of these, comprising this city and county, and which owes its establishment to the persevering efforts of a few individuals, who, in order to succeed, even so far, were compelled to combat the ignorance, the prejudices, and the pecuniary interests of many active and hostile opponents.

But the principles on which these "school districts" are founded, are yet, in the opinion of the committees, extremely defective and inefficient. Their leading feature is pauperism! They are confined exclusively to the children of the poor, while there are, perhaps, thousands of children whose parents are unable to afford for them, a good private education, yet whose standing, professions or connexions in society effectually exclude them from taking the benefit of a poor law. There are great numbers, even of the poorest parents, who hold a dependence on the public bounty to be incompatible with the rights and liberties of an American citizen, and whose deep and cherished consciousness of independence determines them rather to starve the intellect of their offspring, than submit to become the objects of public charity.

There are, also, many poor families, who are totally unable to maintain and clothe their children, while at the schools; and who are compelled to place them, at a very early age, at some kind of labor that may assist in supporting them, or to bind them out as apprentices to relieve themselves entirely of the burden of their maintenance and education, while the practice formerly universal, of schooling apprentices, has, of late years, greatly diminished and is still diminishing.

Another radical and glaring defect in the existing public school system is the very limited amount of instruction it affords, even to the comparatively small number of youth, who enjoy its benefits. It extends, in no case, further than a tolerable proficiency in reading, writing, and arithmetic, and sometimes to a slight acquaintance with geography. Besides these, the girls are taught a few simple branches of industry. A great proportion of scholars, however, from the causes already enumerated, acquire but a very slight and partial knowledge of these branches.

The present public school system, limited as it is to three solitary school districts, makes no provision for the care and instruction of children under five years old. This class of children is numerous, especially among the poor, and it frequently happens that the parents, or parent, (perhaps a widow) whose only resource for a livelihood is her needle or wash tub, is compelled to keep her elder children from the school to take charge of the younger ones, while her own hands are industriously employed in procuring a subsistence for them. Such instances are far from being rare, and form a very prominent and lamentable drawback on the utility of the schools in these districts. The care thus bestowed on infants, is insufficient and very partial. They are frequently exposed to the most pernicious influences and impressions. The seeds of vice, thus early scattered over the infant soil, are too often permitted to ripen, as life advances, till they fill society with violence and outrage, and yield an abundant harvest for magdalens and penitentiaries.

An opinion is entertained by many good and wise persons, and supported to a considerable extent, by actual experiment, that proper schools for supplying a judicious infant training, would effectually prevent much of that vicious depravity of character which penal codes and punishments are vainly intended to counteract. Such schools would, at least, relieve, in a great measure, many indigent parents, from the care of children, which in many cases occupies as much of their time as would be necessary to earn the children a subsistence. They would also afford many youth an opportunity of participating in the benefits of the public schools, who otherwise must, of necessity, be detained from them.

From this view of the public instruction in Pennsylvania, it is manifest that, even in "the school districts," to say nothing of the remainder of the state, a very large proportion of youth are either partially or entirely destitute of education.

It is true the state is not without its colleges and universities, several of which have been fostered with liberal supplies from the public purse. Let it be observed, however, that the funds so applied, have been appropriated exclusively for the benefit of the wealthy, who are thereby enabled to procure a liberal education for their children, upon lower terms than it could otherwise be afforded them. Funds thus expended, may serve to engender an aristocracy of talent, and place knowledge, the chief element of power, in the hands of the privileged few; but can never secure the common prosperity of a nation nor confer intellectual as well as political equality on a people.

The original element of despotism is a monopoly of talent, which consigns the multitude to comparative ignorance, and secures the balance of knowledge on the side of the rich and the rulers. If then the healthy existence of a free government be, as the committee believe, rooted in the will of the American people, it follows as a necessary consequence, of a government based upon that will, that this monopoly should be broken up, and that the means of equal knowledge, (the only security for equal liberty) should be rendered, by legal provision, the common property of all classes.

In a republic, the people constitute the government, and by wielding its powers in accordance with the dictates, either of their intelligence or their ignorance; of their judgment or their caprices, are the makers and the rulers of their own good or evil destiny. They frame the laws and create the institutions, that promote their happiness or produce their destruction. If they be wise and intelligent, no laws but what are just and equal will receive their approbation, or be sustained by their suffrages. If they be ignorant and capricious, they will be deceived by mistaken or designing rulers, into the support of laws that are unequal and unjust.

It appears, therefore, to the committees that there can be no real liberty without a wide diffusion of real intelligence; that the members of a republic, should all be alike instructed in the nature and character of their equal rights and duties, as human beings, and as citizens; and that education, instead of being limited as in our public poor schools, to a simple acquaintance with words and ciphers, should tend, as far as possible, to the production of a just disposition, virtuous habits, and a rational self governing character.

When the committees contemplate their own condition, and that of the great mass of their fellow laborers; when they look around on the glaring inequality of society, they are constrained to believe, that until the means of equal instruction shall be equally secured to all, liberty is but an unmeaning word, and equality an empty shadow, whose substance to be realized must first be planted by an equal education and proper training in the minds, in the habits, in the manners, and in the feelings of the community.

While, however, the committees believe it their duty to exhibit, fully and openly, the main features and principles of a system of education which can alone comport with the spirit of American liberty, and the equal prosperity and happiness of the people, they are not prepared to assert, that the establishment of such a system in its fullness and purity, throughout the state, is by any means attainable at a single step. While they maintain that each human being has an equal right to a full development of all his powers, moral, physical, and intellectual; that the common good of society can never be promoted in its fullness till all shall be equally secured and protected in the enjoyment of this right, and that it is the first great duty of the states, to secure the same to all its members; yet, such is now the degraded state of education in Pennsylvania, compared with what, in the opinion of the committees, education for a free people should be, that they despair of so great a change as must be involved in passing from one to the other, being accomplished suddenly throughout the state. No new system of education could probably be devised with consequences so manifestly beneficial as to awaken at once in the public mind, a general conviction and concurrence in the necessity of its universal adoption.

The committees are aware, also, that it is their duty to consult the views, the feelings, and the prejudices, not of a single district or county merely, but of the state in general. The measure which it is their business to propose, is one designed to be of universal extent and influence, and must, to be successful, be based upon the manifest wishes of nearly the whole commonwealth. It is not, therefore, to what would constitute a perfect education only, but also, to what may be rendered practicable—it is not with a view, exclusively, to the kind of education every child of Pennsylvania ought to have, but likewise to what it is possible, under existing circumstances, views, and prejudices, every child of Pennsylvania may and can have, that they have drawn up a bill or outline of what they deem a system of public education, adapted to the present condition and necessities of the state in general.

The principal points in which the bill for establishing common schools, accompanying this report, differs from the existing system of free schools, are as follows:

1. Its provisions, instead of being limited to three single districts, are designed to extend throughout the commonwealth. 2d. It places the managers of the public schools, immediately under the control and suffrage of the people. 3d. Its benefits and privileges will not, as at present, be limited as an act of charity to the poor alone, but will extend equally and of right to all classes, and be supported at the expense of all. 4th. It lays a foundation for infantile, as well as juvenile instruction. And lastly, it leaves the door open to every possible improvement which human benevolence and ingenuity may be able to introduce.

While, however, the committees would urge the establishment of common elementary schools throughout the state, as comprising, perhaps, the best general system of education which is at present attainable, it is but just to exhibit, also, some of the defects as well as the advantages of such schools; and to suggest such further measures as appear calculated to obviate such defects.

The instruction afforded by common schools, such as are contemplated in the bill for a general system of education, being only elementary, must, of necessity, produce but a very limited development of the human faculties. It would indeed diminish, but could not destroy, the present injurious monopoly of talent. While the higher branches of literature and science remain accessible only to the children of the wealthy, there must still be a balance of knowledge, and with it a "balance of power," in the hands of the privileged few, the rich and the rulers.

Another radical defect in the best system of common schools yet established, will be found in its not being adapted to meet the wants and necessities of those who stand most in need of it. Very many of the poorest parents are totally unable to clothe and maintain their children while at school, and are compelled to employ their time, while yet very young, in aiding to procure a subsistence. In the city of New York, a much more efficient system of education exists than in this city, and common schools have been in successful operation for the last ten or twelve years; yet there are at the present time upwards of 24,000 children between the ages of 5 and 15 years, who attend no schools whatever, and this apparently criminal neglect of attending the schools is traced, chiefly, to the circumstance just mentioned. It is evidently therefore of no avail, how free the schools may be, while those children who stand most in need of them, are, through the necessity of their parents, either retained from them altogether, or withdrawn at an improper age, to assist in procuring a subsistence.

The constitution of this state declares that "the legislature shall provide schools in which the poor may be taught gratis." If this signifies that the poor shall have an opportunity afforded for instruction, it must involve means equal to the end. The poverty of the poor must be no obstruction, otherwise the constitution is a dead letter—nay, worse, an insult on their unfortunate condition and feelings.

The committees, therefore, believe, that one school, at least, should be adopted, calculated to obviate the defects that have been alluded to, and by which the children of all who desire it, may be enabled to procure, at their own expense, a liberal and scientific education. They are of the opinion that a principle fully calculated to secure this object, will be found in a union of agricultural and mechanical with literary and scientific instruction; and they have therefore, in addition to a plan of common elementary schools, drawn up and appended to this report, the substance of a bill providing for the establishment of high schools, or model schools, based upon this principle, which they also present for public deliberation.

Believing, as the committees do, that upon an equal education and proper training to industry, sobriety, and virtue, hangs the liberty and prosperity of the new world, and, perhaps, the ultimate emancipation of the old; and believing, as they do, that the union of industry with literature and science constitutes the only desideratum by which an equal education can be supplied and secured to all classes, they experience the most sincere pleasure in discovering that this good and great principle is gaining in popularity and dominion throughout the world. Not only are institutions of this kind established in France, Prussia, Germany, and Great Britain, in imitation of the original Hofwyl institutions in Switzerland, but in the United States, also, there are several. At Whitesborough, N.Y., there is one with from 30 to 40 pupils; at Princeton, Ky., another containing 80; a third exists at Andover, Mass., that accommodates 60 pupils; a fourth at Maysville, Tenn.; and a fifth has recently been established at Germantown, in this county. At Monmouth, N.J., and at Cincinnati, Ohio, very extensive establishments, based upon this principle, have been or are about commencing.

The Germantown establishment had been commenced only seven months when its first report was made, in November last. The pupils are instructed in literature, the sciences, languages, morals, and manual labor. The latter consists of agriculture, gardening, and some mechanic arts. They are permitted to labor little or much, as their dispositions may incline them or their necessities dictate. The institution, at its commencement, on the

1st of May, 1829, had but four pupils—at the date of the report it had 25. By an estimate made by the board of managers, as early as July last, it appeared that the balances against several of them for board and tuition were but very small, and that some of them, by their labor, had almost cleared their expenses. They generally work from two to five hours per day.

The first institution in which manual labor appears to have been combined with literature and science, was established many years since by Fellenberg, at Hofwyl[3] in the Canton of Bern, Switzerland.

The pupils of this institution, in addition to a common or elementary education, were instructed in almost every branch of literature and science. They were taught agriculture, gardening, and the mechanic arts, and their choice of the latter was greatly facilitated by the numerous workshops on the premises. The elements of drawing, surveying and geometry, botany, mineralogy, music, and athletic exercises formed a part of their amusements.

Hofwyl was an independent, selfgoverning community, regulated by a constitution and bylaws formed by the pupils themselves. It had its code of laws; its council of legislation; its representatives; its civil officers; its treasury. It had its annual elections, and each member had an equal vote; its labors and duties in which all took an equal share. It proposed, debated, and enacted its own laws independent even of Fellenberg himself, and never, writes one of the pupils after he had left it, "never perhaps were laws framed with a more single eye to the public good, nor more strictly obeyed by those who framed them."

The same writer considers this circumstance of forming the school into an independent juvenile republic, as the great lever that raised the moral and social character of the Hofwyl establishment to the height it ultimately attained. It gave birth, he says, to public spirit and to social virtues. It awakened in the young republican an interest in the public welfare, and a zeal for the public good, which might in vain be sought in older but not wiser communities.

There is one point in which the committees believe that the gradual extension and ultimate universal adoption of this system of education will produce a benefit, the value of which no human calculation can ascertain. It is but too well known that the growing effects of intemperance—that assassinator of private peace and public virtue, are in this country terrific; and that this fearful pestilence, unless checked in its career by some more efficient remedy than has yet been resorted to, threatens to annihilate, not only the domestic peace and prosperity of individuals, but also the moral order and political liberties of the nation. No people can long enjoy liberty who resign themselves to the slavery of this tyrant vice. Yet does it appear to the committees, that all efforts to root this moral poison from the constitution of society will prove futile until the trial shall be made upon our youth. When we behold the hundreds, perhaps thousands of youth, who, between the ages of 14 and 21 are daily and nightly seduced around or into the innumerable dens of vice, licensed and unlicensed, that throng our suburbs, we are constrained to believe that in many if not in most cases, the unconquerable habit that destroys the morals, ruins the constitution, sacrifices the character, and at last murders both soul and body of its victim, is first acquired during the thoughtless period of juvenile existence. This plan of education, however, by its almost entire occupation of the time of the pupils, either in labor, study, or recreations; by the superior facilities it affords for engrossing their entire attention, and by its capability of embracing the whole juvenile population, furnishes, we believe, the only rational hope of ultimately averting, the ruin which is threatened by this extensive vice.

The committee are aware that any plan of common and more particularly of equal education that may be offered to the public, is likely to meet with more than an ordinary share of opposition. It is to be expected that political demagogism, professional monopoly, and monied influence, will conspire as hitherto (with several exceptions more or less numerous) they ever have conspired against every thing that has promised to be an equal benefit to the whole population. Nevertheless the appearance that something will now be done for the intellectual as well as every thing for the physical improvement of the state are certainly very promising. The public mind is awake and favorably excited, while the press also is somewhat active on this subject. Our present legislature and chief magistrate appear likewise earnestly desirous of producing a reform in the system of public education, and we believe they are waiting only for the public sentiment to decide on the principles and character of that reform.

When this decision shall be fully made, and openly and firmly supported by the public voice, we doubt not but our representatives will cheerfully give their legislative sanction to those measures of educational reform, which shall appear manifestly based upon the will of the people.

Mechanics' Free Press, February 20, 27, 1830

Notes

Notes to *Preface*

1. Mark A. Lanse argues that a united movement of workers from various crafts "began not with the formation of the Mechanics' Union of Trade Associations in December 1827, but a generation earlier in April 1796" when at least ten unions in Philadelphia "acted in concert, at least for a time." (*Some Degree of Power from Hired Hand to Union Craftsmen in the Printing Trades. 1778-1815*, Fayetteville, Arkansas, 1990, p. 13.)
2. James P. Henderson, "An English Communist, Mr. Gray and His Remarkable Work," *History of Political Economy* 17: (Spring 1985), p. 93.
3. University of Wisconsin WPA, Official Prospect, No. 9441, *The American Labor Press. An Annotated Directory*, with an introduction by John R. Commons, Washington, D.C., 1940, p. iii.
4. Quoted in Ray Ginger, *The Bending Cross: A Biography of Eugene Victor Debs*, New Brunswick, N.J., 1949, p. 221.

Notes to *Essay on William Heighton*

1. *Boston Courier*, Oct. 22, 1834.
2. Steven Russwurm, *Arms, Country, and Class: The Philadelphia Militia and the "Lower Classes" During the American Revolution*, New Brunswick, N.J., 1988, pp. 38, 51, 69, 205, 213.
3. Although the Pennsylvania Constitution of 1776 was the most radical in the country, it did not go as far as the artisans would have liked. Thus, the Committee of Printers, based upon the artisans of Philadelphia, had sought without success to include an article stating: "An enormous proportion of property vested in a few individuals is dangerous to the rights and destructive of the common happiness of mankind and, therefore, every free state hath a right to discourage possession of such property." (Lanse, p. 116.)
4. Philip S. Foner, editor, *We, the Other People*, Urbana, Ill., 1976, pp. 2-5; R. L. Burnhouse, *The Counter-Revolution in Pennsylvania, 1776-1790*, Harrisburg, 1942, pp. 43-68; Elise Rasmusson, "Capital on the Delaware: The Philadelphia Upper Class in Transition, 1789-1801," unpublished Ph.D. dissertation, Brown University, 1962, PP. 42-45.
5. John Bigelow, editor, *The Works of Benjamin Franklin*, New York, 1888)10: 48-51; A.H. Smyth, editor, *The Writings of Benjamin Franklin* (New York, 1905-07) 10: 60, 66-68, 72, 127-29. Henry P. Rosemont, "Benjamin Franklin and the Philadelphia Typo-

graphical Strikers of 1796," *Labor History* 23 (Summer 1981): 399; Lanse, p. 61.

6. Philip S. Foner, editor, *The Democratic-Republican Societies, 1790-1800: A Documentary Source Book*, Westport, Conn., 1976, p. 42; Eugene P. Link, *Democratic-Republican Societies, 1790-1800*, New York, 1942, pp. 71-72. For evidence that some of the Philadelphia mechanics opposed the Democrat-Republican Societies and instead supported the Federalists, *see* Lanse, p. 122.

7. *Ibid.*, p. 126.

8. Richard B. Morris, *Government and Labor in Early America*, New York, 1949, pp. 59, 65, 78-79, 81; John R. Commons and Associates, *History of Labour in the United States* (New York, 1918) 1: 103-10.

9. *Ibid.*, pp. 112-15.

10. Most associations were scientific and humanitarian in purpose and were controlled by conservative upper-class leadership. The Humane Society and the Society for Alleviating the Misery of Public Prisons were two such societies. (See James Mease, M.D., *The Picture of Philadelphia, Giving an Account of its Origin, Increase and Improvements in Arts, Sciences, Manufactures, Commerce and Revenue with a Compendious View of the Societies, Literary, Benevolent, Patriotic and Religious*, Philadelphia, 1811, pp. 264-92.

11. Philip S. Foner, *History of the Labor Movement in the United States* (New York, 1947) 1: 69-70.

12. *Ibid.*, pp. 69-72, 84-87.

13. Richard B. Morris, *Government and Labor in Early America*, New York, 1946, p. 201; Eric Foner, *Tom Paine and Revolutionary America*, New York, 1976, p. 39;

Rollo G. Silver, *The American Printer, 1787-1825*, Charlottesville, Va., 1967, pp. 12-16; David R. Roediger and Philip S. Foner, *Our Own Time: A History of American Labor and the Working Day*, Westport, Conn., 1989, pp. 12-16; Ian M.G. Quimby, "The Cordwainers Protest: A Crisis in Labor Relations," *Winterthur Portfolio* III (1967):86-92; Morison H. Hecksher, "The Organization and Practice of Philadelphia Cabinetmaking Establishments, 1790-1820," M.A. thesis, University of Delaware, 1964, pp. 64-66; Charles F. Montgomery, *American Furniture: The Federal Period in the Henry Francis duPont Winterthur Museum*, New York, 1966, pp. 21-22; Sharon V. Salinger, "Artisans, Journeymen, and the Transformation of Labor in Late Eighteenth Century Philadelphia," *William and Mary Quarterly* 40 (1983): 78-81.

14. John R. Commons and Associates, *A Documentary History of American Industrial Society* (Cleveland, 1910): 29-31.

15. Foner, *History of the Labor Movement in the United States*, vol. I, pp. 120-26. Richard J. Twomey argues that many of the Jeffersonian reformers were hostile to organized labor. When it came to journeymen shoemakers militantly organizing and attempting to exclude workers not belonging to their trade societies from working either alongside them or for a common employer, they balked. Many supported the common law conspiracy law indictment of the shoemakers and other crafts on the grounds that, by forming an exclusive society they were acting against the common good in pursuit of

selfish and illegal gain and power. Moreover, even those who objected to a common law indictment still opposed trade societies. (Richard J. Twomey, *Jacobins and Jeffersonians: Anglo-American Radicalism in the United States, 1790-1920*, New York, 1989), pp. 112-40.

16. Tom W. Smith, "The Dawn of the Urban-Industrial Era: The Social Structure of Philadelphia, 1790-1830," Unpublished Ph.D. dissertation, University of Chicago, 1980, pp. 36-39.

17. J. Thomas Scharf and Thompson Westcott, *History of Philadelphia, 1609-1884*, Philadelphia, 1884, pp. 507-30.

18. Quoted in Smith, *op. cit.*, p. 25.

19. David Montgomery, "The Working Classes of the Pre-Industrial American City, 178?-1830," *Labor History* 9 (Winter 1908): 19.

20. Mease, *op. cit.*, pp. 33-38.

21. Scharf and Westcott, *op. cit.*, pp. 560-64.

22. *Ibid.*, pp. 568-70.

23. *Ibid.*, pp. 581-84; David T. Gilchrist, editor, *The Growth of the Seaport Cities, 1790-1825*, Charlottesville, Va., 1967, pp. 58-60.

24. Matthew Carey, *Addresses of the Philadelphia Society for the Promotion of National Industry*, Philadelphia, 1819, p. v. Although the 1820 industrial census did not inquire as to unemployment, it was widely believed by the investigators that Philadelphia County manufacturers commonly laid off 50-75 percent of their workforce between 1817 and 1820. One correspondent in the *Aurora* claimed the same degree of unemployment as early as 1816, (*Aurora*, Jan. 8, 1816.).

25. Murray N. Rothbard, *The Panic of 1819: Reactions and Policies*, New York, 1962, p. v; *Niles' Register*, Aug. 7, Sept. 4, Oct. 23, 1819; Samuel Rezneck, "The Depression of 1819-21, A Social History," *American Historical Review* 19 (October 1933): 28-29; William A. Sullivan, *The Industrial Worker in Pennsylvania, 1800-1840*, Harrisburg, Pa., 1955, p. 51.

26. Donald R. Adams, "Wage Rates in the Early National Period: Philadelphia, 1785-1830," *Journal of Economic History* 28 (September 1968): 415-16; Laura J. Becker, "The Philadelphia Welfare Cases of the 1820s," *Pennsylvania Magazine of History and Biography* 105(April, 1981): 154-55.

27. Rezneck, *op. cit.*, pp. 38-42; Scharf and Westcott, *op. cit.*, p. 620.

28. *Mechanics' Free Press*, Jan. 26, Aug. 28, 1828.

29. Bruce Laurie, *Working People of Philadelphia, 1800-1850*, Philadelphia, 1980, pp. 10-11.

30. Samuel Hazard, *The Register of Pennsylvania, Philadelphia, 1828-1836*, vol. I, p. 28.

31. Maurice F. Neufeld, "Realms of Thought and Organized Labor in the Age of Jackson," *Labor History* 10 (Winter, 1959): 12-13.

32. Laurie, *op. cit.*, p. 67; William A. Sullivan, "Philadelphia Labor During the Jackson Era," *Pennsylvania History* 15 (1948): 305-20.

33. Howard Oessbam, "The Equalitarian Myth and the American Social Reality: Wealth, Mobility and Equality in the Era of the Common Man," *American Historical Review* 76 (October, 1971): 997; Stuart Blumin, "Mobility and Change in Ante-Bellum Philadelphia," in Stephen Thernstrom and Richard Sennett, editors, *Nineteenth Century Cities*, New Haven, 1969, pp. 195-99.

These and other similar studies reveal how shallow is Professor Gordon S. Wood's statement: "The doubts and anxieties most nineteenth-century Americans expressed were not over inequalities and class oppression in their own midst or over the idea of revolution itself but over the ability of peoples elsewhere successfully to emulate the American Revolution." ("Americans and Revolutionaries," *New York Review of Books*, Sept. 27, 1990, p. 34.)

34. *An Address Delivered before the Mechanics and Working Classes Generally of the City and County of Philadelphia...by the "Unlettered Mechanic."* Philadelphia, 1827, pp. 1-2.

35. Edward Pessen, *Most Uncommon Jacksonians: The Radical Leaders of the Early Labor Movement*, Albany, N.Y., 1967, pp. 54-56.

Northamptonshire was the center of English shoe production and was well known for the strength of its journeymen's organizations. See E.P. Thompson, *The Making of the English Working Class*, New York, 1974, pp. 254-55, 259; Robert W. Malcolmson, "Workers' Combination in Eighteenth-Century England," in Margaret Jacob and James Jacob, eds., *The Origins of Anglo-American Radicalism*, London, 1984, pp. 149-61; Eric J. Hobsbawm and Joan Wallach Scott, "Political Shoemakers," *Past and Present* 89 (1980): 86-114.

36. Nothing much is known about Heighton's early life. What we do know is mainly derived from two studies by Louis H. Arky, "The Mechanics' Union of Trade Associations and the Formation of the Philadelphia Workingmen's Movement," unpublished Ph.D. dissertation, University of Pennsylvania, 1952, and "The Mechanics' Union of Trade Associations and the Formation of the Philadelphia Working-Men's Movement," *Pennsylvania Magazine of History and Biography* 76 (April 1952): 142-76.

37. David Ricardo, *Principles of Economy and Taxation*, London, 1787. On Ricardo's influence in the United States, see Paul K. Conkin, *Prophets of Prosperity: America's First Political Economists*, Bloomington, 1980, pp. 56-80.

38. Esther Lowelthal, *The Ricardian Socialists*, New York, 1911, pp. 133-49; Max Beer, *A History of British Socialism* (London, 1911)1: 143-244.

39. Franklin proposed that the labor time going into the mining of an ounce of silver or the growing of a bushel of corn gave to each its value. "Trade in general being nothing else but the exchange of labour for labour," he wrote, "the value of all things is ... most justly measured by labour."

Jared Starks, ed., *The Works of Benjamin Franklin* (Boston, 1936) 2: 265-67. Commenting later on Franklin's work, Karl Marx wrote that Franklin had clearly "so clearly as to almost be trite" advanced the theory that labor is the source of all value. (*A Contribution to the Critique of Political Economy*, New York, 1970, pp. 52-57.)

40. In Duane's essays, farmers and mechanics were viewed as *sole* producers of wealth, and the income of non-producer merchants, land speculators, and bankers—was viewed as an unjust tax on their labor. (Philadel-

phia *Aurora*, January 1 to March
28, 1907.)

41. Blatchly argued that "if wealth
should produce opulence without the art, labour, or ingenuity
of its proprietor, the opulent
owner must necessarily obtain
his increase from those who exercise art, labour, and ingenuity." Moreover, Blatchly declared, "if (the producer's) industry and labours are the *sole*
cause of the opulence of nations, (then) they are the sole
persons who ought to increase
in opulence." For Blatchly
wealth was not only the product of labor, but a social product as well. He advocated doing
away with private property altogether, subordinating property to society from the beginning. (Cornelius C. Blatchly,
Some Causes of Popular Poverty,
appended to Thomas Bragnan,
The Pleasure of Contemplation,
Philadelphia, 1817), pp. 192-220.

42. Robert Owen spent four days in
Philadelphia in November,
1824. The city gave the English
Utopian Socialist the most en-
thusiastic of his many Ameri-
can receptions, and several
Philadelphia reformers, Gerard
Troost, John Speakman, Dr.
Benjamin Say, and the educational reformer William Mc-
Clure, left the city to participate
in Owen's experimental community in New Harmony, Indiana. In 1826 a group of Philadelphians organized as the
Friendly Association for Mutual
Interests moved to Washington's wartime headquarters at
Valley Forge to begin another
Owenite community.
    Perhaps the outstanding
events in Owen's stay in the
United States were his two
speeches before Congress. On

February 25, 1825, Henry Clay,
who was then Speaker of the
House, called a joint session of
Congress to which he invited
Robert Owen to speak on his
concept of a socialist society.
The newly inaugurated president, John Quincy Adams, was
deeply impressed with Owens
first presentation, and on March
7 of that year he invited Owen to
speak at a second session. Not
only were both houses present,
but members of the Cabinet and
the Supreme Court also attended.
    For Owen's activities in Phila-
delphia and his influence in
America, see Arthur E. Bestor,
Jr., *Backwoods Utopia: The Sectar-
ian and Communitarian Socialism
in America, 1632-1829*, Philadelphia, 1950, pp. 96-97, 100, 107-
08, 110-11, 128-29; J.C.C. Harri-
son, *Quest for the New World:
Robert Owen and the Owenites in
Britain and America*, New York,
1963, passim; W.G. Armytage,
"Owen in America," in Sidney
Pollard and John Salt, eds.,
*Robert Owen, Prophet of the Poor:
Essays in Honor of the Two Hun-
dredth Anniversary of His Birth*,
London, 1970, pp. 214-38.
    Edward Pessen dismisses the
significance of Owen's appearance before Congress as signify-
ing any real advocacy of Utopian Socialism ("Pre-Industrial
New York City Labour Revisited: A Critique of a Recent
Thompson Analysis," *Labour/
Travail* 18 [Fall, 1985]: 237.) For
the full story of Owen's two
speeches before Congress and
the text of his speeches, see
Oakley Johnson, *Robert Owen in
the United States*, New York,
1970.

43. Thompson is famous for having
first put forward the concept of

surplus value upon which Marx would base his system a generation later.

44. New York, 1826.
45. On Gray, *see* J.E. King, "Utopian or Scientific? A Reconsideration of the Ricardian Socialists," *History of Political Economy* 15 (1983): 345-734; John Kimball, *The Economic Doctrines of John Gray, 1779-1882*, Washington, D.C., 1948, and Maurice Dobb, *Theories of Value and Distribution Since Adam Smith*, Cambridge, 1973, pp. 137-47.
46. Ronald Douglas Schultz, "Thought Among the People: Radical Politics, and the Making of Philadelphia's Working Class, 1768-1828," unpublished Ph.D. dissertation, University of California, Los Angeles, 1985, p. 392.
47. John Gray, *A Lecture on Human Happiness*, London, 1825, Philadelphia, 1827, pp. 5, 6, 15, 26-27, 35-36, 37, 39.
48. The existence of a socialist tradition in Philadelphia in the late eighteenth century and early nineteenth century is usually neglected by historians. A major exception are Ronald Douglas Schultz, "Thought Among the People: Popular Thought, Radical Politics, and the Making of Philadelphia's Working Class, 1765-1828," unpublished Ph.D. dissertation, University of California, Los Angeles, 1985, and Tom W. Smith, "The Dawn of the Urban-Industrial Era: The Social Structure of Philadelphia, 1790-1830," unpublished Ph.D, dissertation, University of Chicago, 1980. To a lesser extent is Richard Twomey's "Jacobins and Jeffersonians: Anglo-American Radicalism in the United States, 1790-1820," unpublished Ph.D. dissertation, Northern Illinois University, 1974.

The idea of a socialist commonwealth was first advanced in mid-1802 with the publication of *Equality: A Political Romance*. Published serially in the *Temple of Reason*, a deist newspaper directed at the "middle and lower classes." *Equality* was the work of Dr. James Reynolds. Reynolds was a Dublin physician who had emigrated to Philadelphia in 1794 after serving a prison sentence in Ireland for his ties to the United Irish movement. The novel *Equality* was presented as the travel account of an American visitor to the utopian nation of Litchconia. In contrast to early nineteenth-century Philadelphia, Litchconia was portrayed as nothing less than an ideal community of small producers united in the bonds of true human affection. Reynolds emphasized this contrast in his preface when he wrote, "Happiness is what we are always seeking after (but) where industry is wound up to oppression, Society can never be on a good construction." Unlike Philadelphia's typical 12-to-14-hour workday, Litchconians labored only four hours a day, spending their remaining hours in rest, recreation and study. Moreover, "as befitted an equalitarian society, Litchconia supported no markets but had instead three community warehouses in which were stored food, clothing, and household necessities such as furniture and cooking utensils. These "goods" were distributed among the Litchconians on a regular schedule, thereby eliminating the time-wasting necessity of shopping.

Such a system of distribution, Reynolds argued, "relieved society of the need for unproductive labor so necessary in barbarous countries." "Two men," he wrote, "distribute as much provisions as half the hucksters, grocers, bakers, and butchers in Philadelphia, and two men can distribute as much clothing in one month, as all the Quakers in Pennsylvania could sell in a year.

Reynolds also held out the prospect of marriage and family life freed from the dominance of man over woman and devoid of the separate spheres in which contemporary men and women carried on their daily lives. Political and religious freedom were also guaranteed in Litchconia, although there was no place for an established church or clergy. Even military service was democratic, unlike the case in Revolutionary Philadelphia, no Litchconian could avoid service by paying a fine or hiring a substitute. (James Reynolds, *Equality: A Political Romance*, Philadelphia, 1802, pp.xvii, 8, 9.)

49. *Mechanics' Free Press*, April 12, 1828.

50. The full titles were: *An Address to the Members of Trade Societies and the Working Classes Generally, Being an Exposition of the Relative Situation, Condition, and Future Prospects of Working People in the United States of America, Together with a Suggestion and Outlines of Plan by which they may gradually and indefinitely improve their condition.* By a Fellow-Labourer, Philadelphia, Published by the Author, Young, Printer, 1827, and *An Address Delivered Before the Mechanics and Working Classes Generally, of the City and County of Philadelphia, at the Universalist Church, in Callowhill Street, on Wednesday Evening, November 21, 1827.* By the UNLETTERED MECHANIC, Published by Request of the Mechanics' Delegation. Printed in the Office of the *Mechanics' Gazette*, No. 2, Carter's.

51. (William Heighton), *An Address to the Members of Trade Societies and to the Working Classes Generally*, Philadelphia, 1827, p. 8.

52. *Ibid.*, pp. 1, 3-4.

53. *Ibid.*, p. 10.

54. *Ibid.*, p. 8; *An Address Delivered before the Mechanics and Working Classes Generally of the City and County of Philadelphia...by* the "Unlettered Mechanic," pp. 13-14; David J. Harris, *Socialist Origins in the United States. American Forerunners of Marx, 1817-1832*, Assen, 1966, pp. 82-90; Laurie, *op. cit.*, pp.34, 70, 74-79, 85, 86, 92, 117.

55. *An Address...by* a Fellow-Labourer, p. 14.

56. *Ibid.*, pp. 24, 34; Harris, *op. cit.*, pp. 89-90.

57. *The Principles of Aristocratic Legislation, developed in An Address delivered to the Working People of the district of Southwark, and township of Moyamensing and Passyunk, in the Commissioners' Hall, August 14, 1828* by "An Operative Citizen," Philadelphia, 1828, p. 6.

58. *An Address...by* the "Unlettered Mechanic," pp. 11-16.

59. Arky, *Pennsylvania Magazine of History and Biography, op. cit.*, p. 150.

60. *Ibid.*

61. *An Address...by* the "Unlettered Mechanic," p. 12.

62. *Ibid.*

63. *Ibid.*, p. 14.

64. A Third Address is *The Princi-*
ples of the Aristocratic Legislation,
developed in An Address delivered
to the Working People of the dis-
trict of Southwark, and township
of Mayamensing and Passyuak, in
the Commissioner's Hall, August
14, 1828 by "An Operative Citizen," Philadelphia, 1828. There
is a copy in the Newberry Library, Chicago, Illinois.

65. Copies of the two pamphlets
are in the Library Company of
Philadelphia.

    The fact that the Universalist
Church provided its facilities
for the speech by the "Unlettered Mechanic" is not surprising. "The Universalist Church,"
Lewis H. Arky points out, "had
a reputation for liberalism, if
not heresy."(Ph.D. dissertation,
op. cit., p. 79.)

66. Arky, Ph.D. dissertation, *op. cit.*,
p. 49. Arky writes that "as a
predecessor of Marx on the destiny of the working class,
Heighton seems to have had no
peer." (*Ibid.*, p. 95.) However, he
distorts Marx in writing that
"where Heighton differed
sharply from Marx was his will-
ingness to experiment with the
ballot, but to Marx, reform
through parliamentary maneu-
ver was a sham effort since he
was living in technologically
advanced England and had experienced the repressive action
taken against proletarian movements there and in his native
Germany and in France,"(*Ibid.*,
pp, 95-96.) But Marx repeatedly
emphasized the importance of
working class political action
(and especially independent
working class political action)
for both improvements under
capitalism and as an essential
aspect of the struggle for socialism. He did warn against a rush
into politics before workers had
organized into trade unions to
conduct their battles on the economic front, but he stressed the
importance, once that was
achieved, to wage the class
struggle on both the economic
and political fronts. (See Philip
S. Foner, The Working Men's
Party of the United States: *The*
First Marxist Party in the Ameri-
cas, Minneapolis, 1984.)

67. Laurie, *op. cit.*, p. 76.

68. *Address delivered by* ROBERT OWEN
at a Public Meeting, Held at the
Franklin Institute IN THE CITY OF
PHILADELPHIA, ON MONDAY MORNING,
June 25, 1827, To which is Added
AN EXPOSITION *of the Pecuniary*
Transactions Between That Gen-
tleman, and William McClure.
Philadelphia, 1827, p. 16. Copy
in the British Museum. The *Ad-*
dress was also published in *New*
Harmony Gazette, Aug. 8, 1827.

69. Arky, Ph.D. dissertation, pp. 50-
51. In his two *Addresses* in 1827,
Heighton had made no reference to Robert Owen and his
system. But he soon publicly
announced his support for
Owenite communitarianism, especially in a debate with "Peter
Single" in the *Mechanics' Ga-*
zette. Here Heighton, writing
under the pseudonym of the
"Unlettered Mechanic," defended Owen's system, while
"Peter Single" upheld the existing economic system. Heighton
insisted that not only was
Owen's "superior to every
other organized system of society, but also that it can be made
feasible." However, he also insisted that he favored only "cooperative communities established upon the principles of
mutual interest, equality, and
friendship." He supported his
defense of the Owenite system

by observing that among primitive Christians all things were held in common. While Heighton was sure that at present mankind was not yet ready for this new system, he urged that "our most influential men (be) engaged in preparing the public mind for the duties of such a happy state—a state clearly predicted in the inspired volume, and taught and practiced by Christ and his Apostles." (*Mechanics' Gazette*, Nov. 10, 17, 24, 1827.

70. *An Address...by the "Unlettered Mechanic,"* pp. 13-14.

71. William Heighton, *The Principles of Aristocratic Legislation*, Philadelphia, 1828, p. 13; Heighton, *Address to Trade Societies*, p. 37.

72. Sidney and Beatrice Webb, *History of Trade Unionism in England*, London, 1902, p. 182.

73. *An Address...by the "Unlettered Mechanic,"* pp. 16-17; Commons and Associates, *History of Labor* 1: 185-86.

74. Neufield, *op. cit.*, p. 15.

75. *Mechanics' Gazette*, Jan. 19, Oct. 25, 1827; Philadelphia *Aurora*, Oct. 25, 1828.

76. Arky, Ph.D. thesis, pp. 63-64.

77. *Ibid.*, p. 66.

78. *Ibid.*, p. 68.

79. *Mechanics' Gazette*, Nov. 3, 10, 17, 1827.

80. *Mechanics' Gazette*, Dec. 15, 1827; *Mechanics' Free Press*, June 7, 1828.

81. *Mechanics' Gazette*, Dec. 8, 1827.

82. Arky, Ph.D. dissertation, p. 83.

83. Philip S. Foner, *The Democratic-Republican Societies, 1790-1800*, Westport, Conn., pp. 15-16; William Manning, *The Key of Liberty*, Billerica, Mass., 1922, pp. 66-71; Sean Wilentz, "Exceptionalism. Class Conflict and the American Labor Movement, 1790-1820," *International Labor and Working Class History* 26 (Fall, 1984): 6-7.

84. Helen Sumner views the *Mechanics' Advocate* as "doubtless the first labour paper in the United States, and perhaps in the world...." (John R. Commons and Associates, *History of Labour in the United States* (New York, 1918) 1: 188-89. Actually, the *Mechanics' Advocate* was not really a labor paper, and even if it were, it would not have been the first in the English-speaking world. *The Trades Newspaper and Mechanics' Weekly Journal*, a seven-penny paper started in 1825 by "a committee of delegates from the London trades," seems to be the first labor paper in the English-speaking world. (Beatrice and Sidney Webb, pp. 99-100.)

85. Arky, Ph.D. dissertation, p. 84. The Prospectus for the *Mechanics' Free Press* appeared first in the *Mechanics' Gazette*, but relations between the two papers grew increasingly hostile. The editors of the *Mechanics' Free Press* insisted that they only were the true defenders of the workingmen, standing "unaided and alone, with the torrent of popular prejudice against us...." (*Mechanics' Free Press*, April 12, 1828.) The *Mechanics' Free Press* accused the *Mechanics' Gazette* of having sold out to the enemy because it refused to print the *Address* of the striking house carpenters unless paid. (*Mechanics' Free Press*, June 21, 1828.)

No copies of the *Journeymen's Mechanics' Advocate* have survived, but there is a file of the *Mechanics' Gazette* in the Library of Congress.

86. *Mechanics' Gazette*, Dec. 1, 1827.

87. *Ibid.*
88. Laurie, *op. cit.,* p. 86; Arky, Ph.D. dissertation, pp. 83, 86-87; Dirk Hoerder, "Some Connections between Craft Consciousness and Political Thought among Mechanics, 1820s to 1840s," *Amerikastudien* 30 (no. 3, 1985): 328-31.
89. The *Working Man's Advocate* began its existence on October 31,1829 when the first edition appeared issued by a "Committee of Fifty" in New York City organized early in 1829 to establish a political party and to study the feasibility of publishing a newspaper. The masthead proclaimed: "All children are entitled to equal education, all adults to equal property, and all mankind to equal privileges." While the paper claimed to be "edited by a mechanic," George Henry Evans and his brother, Frederick, actually edited and published the labor weekly. George Henry Evans was born In England, and migrated to the United States when he was fourteen years old. The *Working Man's Advocate* was published in New York City under various titles from 1829 to 1849. (See C.K. McFarland and Robert L. Thistlethwaite, "20 Years of a Successful Labor Paper: The *Working Man's Advocate,* 1829- 49," *Journalism Quarterly* 59 [Spring, 1968]: 35-40.)
90. Reprinted in *Mechanics' Free Press,* June 27, 1829.
91. *Mechanics' Free Press,* April 12, 1828.
92. *Ibid.,* July 25, 1829; Jan. 30, March 6, 13, 1830.
93. *Ibid.,* Nov. 21, 1829.
94. *Ibid.,* Sept. 27, Dec. 13, 20, 27, 1828. In September 1828 the Manayunk cotton manufacturer J.J. Borie announced a 25 per-cent reduction in wage rates. The workers at the mill immediately answered with a strike. When Borie brought in new workers, the factory mule spinners used physical force and the threat of violence to protect their jobs. The arrest and conviction of several spinners for illegal combination and conspiracy contributed to break the strike in December. (Cynthia Jane Skelton, "The Mills of Manayunk. Early Industrialization and Social Conflict in the Philadelphia Region, 1787- 1837," unpublished Ph.D. dissertation, University of California, Los Angeles, 1982, Chapter 6.)
95. Johann Heinrich Pestalozzi (1746-1827) was a Swiss educational reformer who advocated education of the poor and emphasized teaching methods designed to strengthen the student's own abilities. Pestalozzi's method became widely accepted, and most of his principles have been absorbed into modern elementary schools. A school based on Pestalozzian principles existed in Philadelphia for several years. It owed its existence to William Maclure, a Scottish merchant who retired from commerce and emigrated to Philadelphia in the mid-1780s. In Philadelphia, Maclure took up scientific pursuits, performing the nation's first geological survey and helping to found the Philadelphia Academy of Natural Sciences. In 1805 he travelled to France where he met Joseph Neff, a Parisian proponent of Pestalozzian educational reform. Impressed with what he saw, Maclure brought Neff to Philadelphia and helped him establish his Pestalozzian acad-

emy at the Falls of Schuylkill in 1809. Maclure, a leader of the socialist movement in Philadelphia in the early nineteenth century, was convinced that the Pestalozzian system would produce free adults who would use the political knowledge they gain from their education to create an "equal division of property" and thus give true "vigor to the great mass" of the people. (Schulz, *op. cit.*, p. 379.)

96. *Mechanics' Free Press*, March 21, 28, 1829.
97. Heighton, *Principles of Aristocratic Legislation*, p. 6.
98. *Ibid.*, p. 7.
99. *Ibid.*, p. 12.
100. *Ibid.*, p. 14.
101. *Ibid.*, p. 18.
102. For the text of the extract, *see* pp. 59-65.
103. For general discussions of the Working Men's parties of the Jacksonian era, *see* Walter Huggins, *Jacksonian Democracy and the Working Class*, Stanford, 1960; Arthur M. Schlesinger, Jr., *The Age of Jackson*, Boston, 1945; Alden Whitman, *Labor Parties, 1827-1834*, New York, 1943; and Edward Pessen, "The Working Men's Movement of the Jacksonian Era," *Mississippi Valley Historical Review* 43 (December, 1956): 428-43.
104. Among these papers were the *Working Man's Advocate, Daily Sentinel,* and *The Man,* of Now York City (all three edited and published by George Henry Evans); *Free Enquirer* also of New York City; and *Spirit of the Age* (Tuscaloosa, Alabama); *Delaware Free Press* (Wilmington, Delaware); *Farmers' and Mechanics' Advocate* (Charlestown, Indiana); *Liberalist* (New Orleans); *New England Farmer and Mechanic* (Gardiner, Maine);

Working Man's Advocate (Boston); *Village Chronicle* and *Farmers' and Mechanics' Advocate* (Albany, New York); *Workingmen's Bulletin* (Buffalo, New York); *Spirit of the Age* (Rochester, New York), and *Working Men's Union* (Ravenna, Ohio). For a discussion of a key labor paper of the era, *see* C.K. McFarland and Robert L. Thistlethwaite, "20 Years of a Successful Labor Paper: The *Working Man's Advocate*, 1829-49," *Journalism Quarterly* 59 (Spring, 1968): 35-40.

105. *Mechanics' Free Press*, March 21, 1829.
106. Foner, *History of the Labor Movement...*, vol. I, p. 126.
107. *Mechanics' Free Press*, Oct. 31, 1829.
108. "Address of Workingmen of Philadelphia," *Mechanics' Free Press*, July 10, 1830. For the role of the Democratic-Republican Societies in the movement for public education, see Foner, *Democratic-Republican Societies, 1790-1800*, pp. 11, 13-15, 225, 253, 322-23, 426-27, 432.
109. *Mechanics' Free Press*, April 16, 1831. The word "Mind" is followed by an asterisk which is followed by the explanation "Public Mind."
110. *Ibid.*, March 16, 1830.
111. Walter A. Sullivan, "Philadelphia Labor During the Jackson Era," *Pennsylvania History* 15 (October, 1948): 311.
112. Joan L. Stachin, "The Contribution of the American Working Man's Movement to the Establishment of Common Schools in New York and Pennsylvania between 1828 and 1842," unpublished Ph.D. dissertation, Pennsylvania State University, 1963, pp. 64-88.
113. Hazard's *Register* 5: 176; Sullivan, *op. cit.*, p. 319.

114. *Mechanics' Free Press*, Jan. 2, 1830.

115. *Working Man's Advocate*, Feb. 27, March 6, 1830. *Mechanics' Free Press*, Oct. 2, 1830; *Working Man's Advocate*, April 24, 1830.

116. Arthur M. Schlesinger, Jr., *The Age of Jackson*, New York, 1945, pp. 119-21.

117. *Ibid.*, pp. 526-27.

118. Foner, *History of the Labor Movement...*, vol. I. pp. 125-26.

119. Edwin T. Randall, "Imprisonment for Debt in America: Fact and Fiction," *Mississippi Valley Historical Review* 39 (June, 1952): 124-26.

120. See Michael B. Katz, editor, *Education in American History: Readings in the Social Issues*, (New York, 1973) in which there is not a single reference to the influence of the workingmen's movement in advancing the cause of public education. To the revisionists, led by Michael B. Katz and Samuel Bowles, the concept of workingmen's support for public education is a myth. All of which proves that the revisionists have simply not done their homework.
To be sure, some in Philadelphia's upper-class circles felt that public schools could promote law and order, and could prevent the poor from disturbing the city's calm with their "vicious habits." But to tax conscious upper and middle-class Philadelphians the idea of paying for the education of the poor was anathema. Moreover, they believed that education would "spoil" the poor and make them unfit for their station in society. (*See* Jacqueline Reusser Reinier, "Attitudes toward and Practices of Child-Rearing: Philadelphia, 1790 to 1830," unpublished Ph.D, dissertation, University of California, Berkeley, 1977, pp. 8-9.)

121. *Mechanics' Gazette*, Jan. 9, 1828.

122. *Mechanics' Free Press*, Aug. 16, 1828.

123. Whitman, *op. cit.*, p. 23.

124. *Mechanics' Free Press*, July 5, 1828.

125. *Ibid.*

126. Arky, Ph.D. dissertation, p. 114.

127. *Poulson's American Daily Advertiser*, May 28, 1828; Philip S. Klein, *Pennsylvania Politics, 1817-1832: A Game Without Rules*, Philadelphia, 1940, pp. 119-42.

128. The city legislature consisted of twenty Common Council members and fifteen Select Council members. Members of the former body were elected annually while the members of the latter served for three years and vacated their seats in rotation so that one third of them were elected each year. (J. Thompson Scharf, *History of Philadelphia* (Philadelphia, 1883)3: 1703.

129. *Mechanics' Free Press*, May 31, Aug. 16, 1828.

130. *Ibid.*, June 21, Aug. 9, 23, 1828.

131. Arky, Ph.D. thesis, pp. 120-21; *Democratic Press*, Aug. 13, 1828.

132. The sole copy, with a new introduction by William Heighton, is deposited in the Newberry Library, Chicago, *See* also *Mechanics' Free Press*, Aug. 16, Oct. 11, 1828.

133. *Principles of Aristocratic Legislation*, pp. 13-16.

134. Arky, Ph.D. thesis, p. 128,

135. *Mechanics' Free Press*, April 12, 1828.

136. *Ibid.*, Sept. 13, 1828. "Jacksonian Democracy," Arthur Schlesinger, Jr., has written recently, "included opportunists out for a fast buck as well as radical democrats committed to pure

doctrine." ("The Age of Jackson." *New York Review of Books*, Dec. 7, 1989, p. 49. It was the presence of the former in the Working Men's Party that disturbed Heighton.

137. *Ibid.*
138. *Ibid.*
139. *Ibid.*, Oct. 18, 25, 1828.
140. Arky, Ph.D. thesis, p. 131.
141. *Mechanics' Free Press*, Oct. 18, 1828.
142. *Ibid.*
143. Schultz, *op. cit.*, p. 408.
144. Schlesinger, Jr., "The Age of Jackson," p. 47.
145. Schultz, *op. cit.*, p. 408.
146. *Mechanics' Free Press*, Nov. 1, 1828.
147. Sullivan, "Philadelphia Labor in Jackson Era," p. 306.
148. *Ibid.*; *Poulson's American Daily Advertiser*, Feb. 27, 1829.
149. Matthew Carey, *Appeal to the Wealthy of the Land*, Philadelphia, 1830, 3rd Edition, pp. 3-5.
150. Helen L. Sumner, "History of Women in Industry in the United States," in "Report on Condition of Woman and Child Wage Earners in the United States," *United States Bureau of Labor* (Washington, D.C., 1910) 9: 125.
151. Matthew Carey, *Plea for the Poor*, Philadelphia, 1829, pp. 6-7; Sullivan, "Philadelphia Labor in Jackson Era," p. 306.
152. Arky, Ph.D. thesis, p. 141.
153. *Mechanics' Free Press*, Nov. 29, 1828.
154. *Ibid.*, Nov. 1, 29, 1828.
155. Foner, *History of Labor Movement...*, I: 128.
156. For the role of Frances Wright in the labor movement of the Jacksonian era, *see Ibid.*, pp. 129-32, 136-38; and Edward Pessen, *Most Uncommon Jacksonians: The Radical Leaders of the Early Labor Movement*, Albany, N.Y., 1967,

pp. 31, 56, 63, 70, 73, 140, 143, 185.
157. The second address was delivered on the Fourth of July, 1829 at the Walnut Street Theatre. See, *Address to the People of Philadelphia in the Walnut Street Theatre on the Morning of the Fourth of July, Common Era 1829, and the Fifty-fourth year of Independence by Frances Wright*, New York, 1829.
158. Arky, Ph.D. thesis, p. 79.
159. *Mechanics' Free Press*, June 27, 1829.
160. *Ibid.*, Oct. 17, 1829; Arky, Ph.D, thesis, p. 145.
161. Only four unions were reported sending delegates to the final meeting. (John R. Commons and Associates, *A Documentary History of American Industrial Society* (Cleveland, 1910)5: 76.
162. William Russell, "Education and the Working Class: The Expansion of Public Education during the Transition to Capitalism," unpublished Ph.D. thesis, University of Cincinnati, 1981, p. 271.
163. *Mechanics' Free Press*, Feb. 20, 1830.
164. *Ibid.*
165. Russell, *op. cit.*, p. 277.
166. *Working Man's Advocate*, June 7, 1830; Foner, *History of Labor Movement...*, I: 128-29.
167. *Mechanics' Free Press*, May 30, 1830.
168. Quoted in Pessen, *Some Uncommon Jacksonians*, pp. 28-29.
169. *Mechanics' Free Press*, Oct, 9, 1830.
170. Simpson grew up in the shadow of the Bank of the United States, where his father was a chief cashier. As a young man he followed in his father's footsteps, becoming a note clerk in the Second Bank of the United States. Then in 1818 he

resigned and exposed the incompetence and malfeasance of the bank's director in the pages of the *Aurora*.

In *The Working Man's Manual* Simpson insisted: "Labor is the source of wealth, and industry, the arbiter of its distribution." But as he looked around him, he found this principle everywhere violated. "They (who) do all the work, elect all the public functionaries, fight all the battles, gain all victories, cause all our enjoyment to flow upon us," he noted, "still remain destitute, deprived of the frugal store of competence which ought to be the reward of industry." Instead it was the capitalists who "live and grow rich by the labour of others." Simpson explained that "Capital is naturally a tyrant; always standing on the alert to grind down the more the operative who lives from hand to mouth, and who must sell (his labour) because he must eat." There was "no means other than this fraud, monopoly, and unjust distribution of labour" he concluded, by which the capitalist could "grow rich and the industrious majority remain poor." (Stephen Simpson, *The Workingmen's Manual: A New Theory of Political Economy for the Principle of Production the Source of Wealth*, Philadelphia, 1831, pp. 8, 29, 48, 69, 70.

Simpson's ideas are set forth in Edward Pessen, "The Ideology of Stephen Simpson, Upper-Class Champion of the Early Philadelphia Workingmen's Movement," *Pennsylvania History* 22 (1955): 328-40; Edward Pessen, *Most Uncommon Jacksonians: The Radical Leaders of the Early Labor Movement*, Al-

bany, N.Y., 1967, pp. 75-78; Joseph Dorfman, *The Economic Mind in American Civilization, 1606-1865* (New York, 1946) II: 645-48.

For a critical view of Stephen Simpson, see Pessen, *Uncommon Jacksonians*, pp. 75-77, and Arky, Ph.D. thesis, pp. 146-47. For a more sympathetic view, see Schlesinger, Jr., *The Age of Jackson*, pp. 195-98. Schlesinger, however, is incorrect in describing Simpson as the "leading Jacksonian of the Philadelphia Working Men's Party, 1828-1831." (*Ibid.*, p. 201.)

171. *Mechanics' Free Press*, Oct. 9, 1830.

172. *Ibid.*, Oct. 16, 1830; Foner, *History of the Labor Movement*, vol. I, p. 129; Leonard Bernstein, "The Working People of Philadelphia, From Colonial Times to the General Strike of 1835," *Pennsylvania Magazine of History and Biography* 74 (1950): 332-33.

173. *Mechanics' Free Press*, Oct. 12, 1830.

174. *Ibid.*, Oct, 29, 1830, March 2, 1831.

175. Arky, Ph.D. thesis, pp. 160-62.

176. William Heighton to George L. Stearns, February 27, 1865, reprinted in (Anon.), *The Equality of All Men before the Law Claimed and Defended*, Boston, 1865, pp. 42-43.

177. The Working Men's Party's candidates running for city office without endorsement by either major party received less than 420 votes each, although candidates for state assembly polled from 1,316 to 1,800 votes. (*Mechanics' Free Press*, March 2, 9, 16, 1831.)

178. A. Fuller Spaulding in *Labour/Travail* 40 (Number 2, 1985): 161-62. For Tom Paine's influence on the labor move-

ment of the Jacksonian era, see Mark A. Lanse, "The 'Unwashed' Infidelity : Thomas Paine and the Early New York City Labor History," *Labor History* 27 (Summer, 1986): 385-403.

179. *Working Man's Advocate*, Dec. 11, 1830.

180. *Mechanics' Free Press*, March 19, 1831.

181. Isaac Sharpless, *Two Centuries of Pennsylvania History*, Philadelphia, 1900, p. 304; Donald Scott McPherson, "The Fight Against Free Schools in Pennsylvania: Popular Opposition to the Common School System, 1834-1874," unpublished Ph.D. dissertation, University of Pittsburgh, 1977, pp. 38-41; Sullivan, "Philadelphia labor During the Jackson Era," pp. 319-20.

The class composition of both the leaders and the supporters of the Working Men's Party of Philadelphia has become the object of debate. William A. Sullivan and George Rogers Taylor have rejected the View that the Working Men's Party of Philadelphia was an authentic working class movement or a bona fide organization battling in the interest of the wage-earners. Rather, they insist, its name was spurious, employed by clever politicians who used the nomenclature to confuse workers as to their real objectives. But Louis A. Arky and Edward Pessen argue that the Working Men's Party of Philadelphia was a distinct working-class movement. Arky found that a high percentage of the Party's early leaders, more than 75 percent, in fact, were workers, mostly artisans. They included cordwainers, brushmakers, tailors, printers, hatters, chairmakers, carriers, tin-plate

workers, carpenters, brickmakers, and a plasterer. Edward Pessen notes that "the men who actually ran the party were themselves workers. Pessen, moreover, points out that the program of the Party reflected the real needs of the workers of Philadelphia, even though they did not, as some critics argue, sufficiently emphasize economic issues. Workingmen, he correctly points out, "had needs that ranged beyond the economic."

See William A. Sullivan, *The Industrial Worker in Pennsylvania*, Harrisburg, Pa., 1955, pp. 151-55; George R. Taylor in Preface to new edition of John R. Commons and Associates, *A Documentary History of the American Industrial Society* (New York, 1962) 5: VI-VII; Louis H. Arky, Ph.D. thesis, pp. 144-45; Edward Pessen, "The Working Men's Party Revisited," pp. 208-09, 213.

Sean Wilentz emphasizes the distinction between what he calls "the radical Working Men's movement" and "The entrepreneurial Working Men's Party." (*Chants Democratic: New York City and the Rise of the American Working Class, 1788-1850*, New York, 1984, p. 212. On the other hand, Arthur Schlesinger, Jr. writes: "If many of the self-styled 'workingmen' of Jackson's days were not, in fact, workers at all but small proprietors on the way up, why would they define themselves as members of the working class and carry on so about the rich?" ("The Age of Jackson," p. 49.)

182. Sullivan, *op. cit.*, p. 156.

Notes to *An Address Delivered before the Mechanics and Working Classes Generally ... by the "Unlettered Mechanic"*

1. The reference is to the Declaration of Independence.
2. Here Heighton projects the idea of surplus value, which was defined by Marx as "congealed labor," for which workers had not been paid. Marx argued that the profit system deprived its real creators of their just due.
3. For the establishment of the Mechanics' Library Company, *see* pp. 25-26, 87-88.
4. For a discussion of the *Mechanics' Gazette*, see p. 26.

Notes to *Report of the Working Men's Committee on Public Education*

1. The committee was appointed at a meeting of the workingmen, and its report, "after much deliberation and some amendments made," was unanimously adopted at a meeting of the "friends of general and equal education." The discussion of the report took three evenings, February 4, 8, and 11, 1830.
2. A state law had authorized county establishment of public schools in 1812, but the war had interfered with its execution. In 1817 about 49,000 children of poor parents were still being maintained by county funds at various private schools. In the desire to reduce expenses, wealthy Philadelphians favored the introduction of the Lancasterian, or tutorial, system of monitoring many students by a single teacher. Under this plan costs could be lowered from $10.00 or $12.00 to less than $4.00 per pupil per year. By 1818 the Pennsylvania Society for the Promotion of Public Economy was promoting adoption of the Lancasterian plan, based on the idea of the British educator, Joseph Lancaster. The method was adopted by the public school system since it was so economical, and by the end of 1818, 2,845 "children of indigent parents" were receiving instruction under the Lancasterian system. This number doubled in three years. (See Charles Calvert Ellis, "Lancasterian Schools in Philadelphia," unpublished Ph.D. thesis, University of Pennsylvania, 1907.)
3. Swiss educator Emmanuel van Fellenberg established a school at Hofwyl where he sought to combine industry with education. Robert Owen, the British Utopian Socialist, sent his sons, Robert Dale and William, to be educated at the school. This manual labor movement had considerable influence in the United States.

Index

abolition of imprisonment for debt, 35
abolition of licensed monopoly, 33
Adams, John Quincy, 39, 111
Age of Jackson, reevaluation of, ii-iii
American Disciples of Marx: From the Age of Jackson to the Progressive Era, ii
Arky, Louis, iii, 21, 114, 139, 180
Arms, Country, and Class: The Philadelphia Militia and the Lower Sort During the American Revolution, 1
artisans, republican, ii
Association for the Protection of Industry and the Production of Popular Instruction, 36
Associators, 108

Bancroft, George, 1
banks, opposition to, 36-37
Battle of New Orleans, 51
Bill of Rights, 8
Black workers, 30
Blair, Joseph L., ii
Blatchly, Cornelius C., 12, 111
Borie, J. J., 116
Borie, Legueren & Keating, 10
Bowles, Samuel, 118
Bragman, Thomas, iii
Bylesby, Langdon, 13

Carey, Matthew, 9, 35, 43-44
carpenters, 6
chair makers, 6-7
Chants Democratic: New York City and the Rise of the American Working Class, 1788-1850, ii
chartered monopolies, opposition to, 36-37
Class and Power Before the Civil War, i
class contradictions, 11
Clay, Henry, iii
clergy, 82
Committee of Printers, 7, 107
Committees of Vigilance, 44
Commons, John R., iii; and Associates, i, ii
Communitarianism, 114-15
Congress, in Joint Session to hear Robert Owen, iii

conspiracy cases, 8, 108-09
cordwainers, i, 7-8, 30

Debs, Eugene Victor, iii
Declaration of Independence, 18, 34, 74-75
Democratic-Republican Societies, 14, 108, 117
Democratic Society of Pennsylvania, 4
depression of 1818-19, 9, 109
Duane, William John, 12, 43, 110-11

education, *see* public education
elections, of 1828, 39-43; of 1829, 43-50; of 1830, 50-52; of 1831, 120
electoral system, 38-39
Embargo Act of 1807, 8
Engels, Frederick, 12
Equality: A Political Romance, 112-13
Evans, Frederick, 116
Evans, George Henry, 116

Federal Constitution, 8
Federal Society of Chair Makers, 6-7
Federalist Party, 51
Federalists, 3, 42, 51
Four Alls, 4
Franklin, Benjamin, denounces upper classes, 3; on labor theory of value, 12, 110; roll in formation of printers' union, 3; supports French Revolution, 3; sympathizes with wage earners, 3
Franklin Society, 2-3
Friendly Assn. of Mutual Interests, 111

gambling, 88
Genius of Universal Emancipation, The, 30
Glasgow, James, 40-41
Gray, John, 13-15, 31
Greece, 70

Harris, David J., iii
Hazard's Register, 10, 36
Heighton, William, biog. info, i, ii, 10-12; and Black workers, 30; on capitalism, 81-82; and communitarianism, 114-15; contributions summarized, i, ii, 53-55, 114; and David Ricardo, i, ii,

12; and elections—1828, 42-43, 1829, 43-50, 1830, 50-53; and John Gray, 13-15; and labor movement—1st labor paper, i, 26; 1st labor party, i, 84-85, 91-95; labor creates all value, 12, 69-70; and political action, 32-32; rights and status of, 18-19, 72-75. on legislators, 62, 79-81; and Phila. Working Men's Party, 33-55; political thought of, 37-38; and public education, 18-19, 47; and radical reconstruc tion, 53; and Robert Owen, 21; and shorter hours, 60-61; and trade union unity, 86-87; and women workers, 30; on working class, status of, 59-61, 70-71, 72-73, 79; and workingman's library, 25-26, 64, 87-88; writings of, 27-29, 96-106

Herreshoff, David, ii
Henderson, James P., ii
Hofwyl, 104, 122
hours of labor, 4-6, 60-61
Humane Society, 108

imprisonment for debt, 36
Inquiry into the Principles of the Distribution of Wealth, 13
Jackson, Andrew, 38, 42, 43, 51
Jacksonian democracy, nature of, xi, 18-19
Jeffersonians, and organized labor, 108-09
judicial class, 80-81

Katz, Micheal B., 118
Key of Liberty, 26
Kline, William O., 42

labor, and education, 33-36; labor journalism, iii, 33, 115-17; solidarity and, 7; labor theory of value, 12, 69-70; *see also* under Heighton, William
Lane, Mark A., 107
lectures, by Heighton, on Existing Evils and Their Remedy, 46; on Human Happiness, 13, 15, 31
Levellers, 84
Lichtonia, 112-13

McAllister, James, 41
Maclure, William, 116-17
Manayunk, 10
Manning, William, 26
Marx, Karl, 12, 110, 112, 114, 122
mechanics, role in Amer. Revolution, 1-3; in political societies, 4

Mechanics' Advocate, 26, 115
Mechanics' Free Press, i, iii, 9, 13, 26, 27, 30, 35, 79, 115
Mechanics' Gazette, 27-28, 114, 115
Mechanics of Baltimore: Workers and Politics in the Age of Revolution, ii
Mechanics' Library Company of Phila., 25-28
mechanics' lien law, 36, 55
Mechanics' Union of Trade Associations, iii, 22-23, 24-25, 39, 86-87, 119, 127
merchant capitalists, 4-5, 9, 10
Mifflin, Thomas, 2
militia system, 33, 36
Modest Inquiry into the Nature and Necessity of Paper Currency, A, 12
Montgomery, David, 8-9
Most Uncommon Jacksonians: The Radical Leaders of the Early Labor Movement, iii
Mutual Benefit Societies, 5

Neff, Joseph, 116-17
New Harmony, iii
New York *Working Man's Advocate*, 28-29
Non-Intercourse Acts, 8

official labor, 71-72
"Old Hickory," 143
Owen, Robert, 13, 20-25, 46, 111

Paine, Thomas, 13, 53, 120-21
"pauper schools," 11, 33
Pennsylvania, constitution of 1776, 2-3, 107; of 1790, 3; education in, status of, 35; public schools established, 55
Perfectionists' Radical Social Thought in the North, 1815-1860, The, ii
Pessen, Edward, i, iii, 120-21
Pestalozzi, Johann Heinrich, 116
Pestalozzian educational reforms, 31
Philadelphia, socialist tradition in, 111-12; status of education in, 35; unemployment in, 9, 43-44, 109; working class in, 1-2, 5-11, 74-5
Philadelphia Academy of Natural Science, 86
Philadelphia *Argus*, 7
Philadelphia *Aurora and General Advertiser*, 8, 12
Philadelphia Cabinet and Chair-Maker's Book of Prices, The, 6-7
Philadelphia Working Men's Party, 33-52
Pleasure of Contemplation, The, iii
poems, 31, 35

Principles of Aristocratic Legislation..., 40-41
public education, Heighton fights for, 34-36, 96-106; labor's role in, ii; revisionist view of, 118
"Report of the Working Men's Committee for Publication," 47-50, 96-106, 122
Republican Assn. of the Working Men (Phila.), 45, 47, 53
Reynolds, James, 112-13
Ricardian Socialists, i, 11-15, 21-30
Ricardo, David, 12, 110
"Rights of the Working People and the Cause of Universal Education, The," 47
Russwurm, Steve, 1, 2

Salinger, Sharon V., 7
Saposs, David T., 4
Say, Benjamin, iii
Schlesinger, Arthur, Jr., 118-19, 120, 121
Second Bank of the United States, 119-20
shoemakers. *see* cordwainers
Simpson, Stephen, 51-2, 119-20
Smith, Adam, 12
Socialist Origins in the United States: Forerunners of Marx, 1817-1832, iii
Social Theories of Jacksonian Democracy: Representative Writings of the Period, 1825-1850, ii
Society for Alleviating the Misery of Public Prisons, 108
Some Causes of Popular Poverty, 12, 112
Spaulding, A. Fuller, 53
Speakman, John, iii
state gaurdianship, 46
Steffens, Charles P., ii
strikes: cabinetmakers (1795), 7; carpenters (1791), 6; cordwainers, 7-8; printers (1786), 6; textile workers (1828), 116
suffrage, 63; right of, endangered, 82-83
Sullivan, William A., 55, 121
Sumner, Helen, 115

surplus value, 77, 112, 122
sympathy strikes, 8

Taylor, George Rogers, 121
Temple of Reason, 112
theological class, 80-81
Thirteenth Amendment, 53
Thompson, Edward, 111-12
Thompson, William, 13
Tocqueville, Alexis de, i
Tories, 2
Trades Newspaper and Mechanics' Weekly Journal, The, 115
trade unions, emerge in Phila., 5-8; *see also* strikes, labor, workingclass
Troost, Gerard, iii
Tworney, Richard J., 108
Unemployment, 7, 9, 43-4, 109
unequal taxation, 37
United Irish movement, 110
Universalist Church, 114
"universal suffrage," Heighton exposes, 63
Utopian Socialism, 20-21, 46

van Fellenberg, Emanuel, 104, 122
Vaux, Robert, 35
Veysey, Laurence, ii

War Department, 44
ward political clubs, 44-45
Wilentz, Sean, ii, 121
women workers, 10, 30, 44
Wood, Gordon S., 110
workers' parties, 33-53
workingclass, 1, 4-11; conditions of, 59-61, 72-3, 75
Working Man's Advocate, 116
workingmen's library, 19, 25, 64
Working Men's Committee on Public Education, Report of, 96-106
Workingmen's Manual: A New Theory of Political Economy..., 51-2, 120
Working Men's Party of Phila., 91-95; contributions of, 75; debate over composition of, 121; disappears, 53; elections of 1828-1831, 42-53
Wright, Frances, 45-6, 52, 119